# My Russian Way

*a spiritual autobiography*

## Alexandre Havard

*Translated from French and Russian
by Anthony T. Salvia*

2016

Design and Production by Jerry Anderson

Printed in Canada.

# PREFACE

"Books we write about ourselves," remarks Nikolai Berdyaev[1] in his autobiography, "are very egocentric." He says that while autobiographers mention other people and events, they are concerned to speak mainly about themselves. He says of his own autobiography, "This book is openly and consciously egocentric. But this egocentrism, about which there is always something repulsive, is here compensated for by the fact that my life and my fate are, for me, the object of philosophical knowledge."[2]

Berdyaev is a philosopher. I am a teacher. I teach virtuous leadership and, in doing so, assert, every bit as emphatically as Berdyaev, the importance of self-knowledge. Without it and without awareness of our vocation, mission, talents and weaknesses, leading virtuously would be impossible.

There comes a time in life for taking stock. Not only to give thanks to God for gifts received and ask forgiveness for our sins, but also to become more deeply aware of our own essence and remain true to it to the end. This essence has nothing to do with our dreams or ambitions. It is God's eternal plan for each one of us.

Delving into one's past and discerning its meaning are tasks everyone should undertake—which is not to say we are all bound to publish the results. But if friends, family members and students insist, why should one refuse?

I decided not to refuse and set myself to the task.

*Moscow, October 13, 2013*

*To my father*

*The past is linked with the present by an
unbroken chain of events flowing one out of
another. It seemed to him … that when he
touched one end the other quivered.*

Anton Chekhov, "The Student"

# CONTENTS

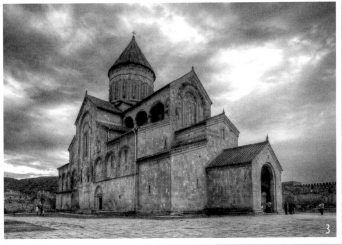

1  Saint Nino, Apostle and
   Enlightener of Georgia
   (280-335 A.D.)

2  My maternal grandfather
   Artschil Gedevanishvili.
   Tbilisi, 1911.

3  The Cathedral of the Twelve
   Apostles in Mtskheta, Georgia.

# THE PASSIONATE ONES

Tbilisi, Georgia, 1921. The Communists take power. Artschil Gedevanishvili, a 22-year-old student of noble descent, fears for the future of his country.

In 1927, the regime grows considerably more repressive. Artschil choses liberty: In the course of that year, he flees the Soviet hell-state leaving behind a mother, a sister and two brothers. His elder brother and brother-in-law will be executed by firing squad in 1937. His younger brother, a soldier on the front, will go missing in action during World War II. His sister, he will not see until 40 years later—in 1967. His mother, he will never see again.

Artschil Gedevanishvili is my maternal grandfather.

☆

The Gedevanishvilis enter history on Golgotha in the first century of the Christian era. Two brothers, Gedeon and Elioz—Jews from the ancient Georgian capital of Mtskheta—serve in the Roman army. They crucify a man condemned to death, a fellow Jew, who claims to be the Son of God. They cast lots for his impressive cloak, woven in a single piece by his mother who, weeping and yet serene, is present at the

1

foot of the cross. The Crucifixion leaves a wound in their hearts that would never heal; they quit the army and return to Georgia.[3]

☆

Three centuries later, a young girl with the sweet name of Nino—who was originally from Cappadocia (Asia Minor) and a cousin of Saint George and niece of the Patriarch of Jerusalem—travels to Rome. There, encouraged by the successor to Saint Peter, she decides to go to Georgia to preach the Gospel. She has known since childhood that the cloak of Christ was to be found at the City of Mtskheta. The Virgin Mary appears to her, confirms her in her mission and offers her a cross made from a grapevine: the famous Cross of Saint Nino, which would accompany her until death. By her example, preaching and miracles, Nino converts her adopted country to Christianity.

In 334, she chooses a site in Mtskheta located over the reliquary containing the Cloak of Christ, at the confluence of the Mtkvari and Aragvi Rivers, for the construction of Georgia's first church. The Georgian King Mirian III commissions the building of the church, which would become known as the Cathedral of the Twelve Apostles. Owing to the presence of the Holy Cloak, the cathedral quickly becomes the world's most venerated Christian shrine, after the Church of the Holy Sepulcher in Jerusalem.

The descendants of Gedeon and Elioz—the Gedevanishvilis—were charged by royal decree with protecting the cloak and the cathedral. On my family's coat of arms are the Ten Commandments engraved on two tablets (indicative of our Jewish origins), the cloak of Christ, the episcopal miter and scepter, the sword and the banner, and the keys to the cathedral at Mtskheta.

☆

Fleeing the Communists in the Soviet Union, Artschil Gedevanishvili goes to Paris where he earns a living as a fur-

2

niture mover. One day at work, he meets Madeleine Ducroq, the daughter of a general in the French army.

Madeleine is crazy about him. Her family is furious: One does not marry an immigrant, especially one who is not Catholic and has not shed a drop of blood for France!

Artschil has to wait 10 years in order to marry the one he loves.

☆

As a couple, they are unique. They have a fiery temperament and a manly will. They thirst for greatness.

They are guided more by intuition than logical thinking. They are motivated by a sense of dignity.

Everything about this couple harmonizes. He is the quintessence of Georgia, she the quintessence of France.

They are a Christian couple. They are poor.

☆

Madeleine is a woman of uncommon sincerity. She thinks aloud. She has no secrets.

She is frequently seen in church. It was she who taught me to pray.

Madeleine. I see her in the kitchen, her apron about her waist. She speaks with a strong voice because she speaks for all humanity. She tells us the history of the bold and courageous men and women who made France a great and marvelous nation. She also speaks to us about her brother, Paul, who died at the second battle of the Marne in 1918. He was 28 years old.

Madeleine is the daughter of a soldier; she cannot stand the lukewarm, the indecisive, the disloyal.

☆

Artschil is all masculine tenderness and human warmth. When he would see us, his grandchildren, he would devour us with his smile.

This man is a patriarch. When I think of the fatherhood of

God, I think of my Georgian grandfather.

I see him again today dressed in his *cherkeska*,[4] his elegant bandolier and his warrior's knife suspended from his belt. His look is filled with an infinite sorrow, the sorrow of separation—forever—from his country and the people he loves. But what pride is in that look, what dignity and nobility!

For Artschil, the past, present and future are one and the same. In him lives an entire people and its history. Artschil is not an "individual" but a person: His life cannot be considered in isolation, but only in relation to the lives of others. His life has meaning only to the extent it is perpetuated in them.

Artschil abominates Rousseauean individualism and Cartesian rationalism. But he loves France. Above all, he loves Paris, which for him is the embodiment of civilization.

He dies of leukemia in 1971 in Paris. Before leaving us, he confesses his sins to Father Elie Melia, rector of the Orthodox parish of Saint Nino, and receives the Body and Blood of Christ. The last words he speaks are to his daughter, my mother: "Return to Georgia as soon as the country is liberated from the Communist yoke and take care of our people."

I am nine years old. My suffering is immense, almost unbearable. More than a grandfather, a father has left us. He is the foundation, the memory and the dignity of the whole family.

# THE GENTLE ONES

If the Gedevanishvilis are preeminent on the maternal side of the family, that distinction belongs to the Dianins on the paternal side.

☆

Pavel Afanasevich Dianin is the first Dianin about whom much is known. An Orthodox priest, he became, in 1840, the pastor of the Church of the Transfiguration in Davydovo, several miles from Vladimir,[5] the city that gave its name to the much venerated icon, the Vladimirskaya Mother of God. He has five children, all of them boys.

☆

One of these children, Aleksandr, is my great-grandfather. He studied medicine and chemistry in St. Petersburg, where he served as an assistant to professor Aleksandr Borodin. By a twist of fate, Borodin is a distant relative—not of Aleksandr Dianin, but on my mother's side: He is the illegitimate son of Luka Gedevanishvili, a Georgian prince.

Borodin is more than a chemist—he is also a renowned musician and composer. Dianin invites him to stay at the family's *izba*[6] in Davydovo. There, over three summers, Borodin writes

4  Pavel Afanasevich Dianin,
   grandfather of my paternal
   grandfather and Orthodox
   priest.

6  The Church of the
   Transfiguration in Davydovo,
   where Pavel Afanasievich
   served as pastor.

5  The izba of the Dianin
   family in Davydovo.

his famous opera, "Prince Igor," a masterpiece inspired by Russian folk traditions, although he dies before completing the work.

Borodin is fascinated by Pavel Afanasevich's personality. "The embodiment of simplicity, kindness and warmth, such as I can imagine only in a man who comes from the people, but never left the people," Borodin writes to Dianin. "How much in him is innate, fine, genuine—not bourgeois European—sensitivity, kindness, simplicity without any constraint, helpfulness without servility."[7]

Borodin is also fascinated by the place. "How good it is to live there! I have never encountered a healthier place than Davydovo," he writes in another letter to Dianin. "What freedom! What freedom!"[8]

☆

Aleksandr Dianin marries Elizabeth, the adopted daughter of Aleksandr Borodin. They will have a son, Sergei, whose godfather will be the composer Nikolai Rimsky-Korsakov, who completes Borodin's "Prince Igor."

☆

Aleksandr Dianin is a great chemist. In 1891, on the strength of his discovery of bisphenol A—a carbon-based synthetic compound used in epoxy resins—he succeeds his father-in-law as chairman of the Chemistry Department at the Imperial Medical-Surgical Academy in St. Petersburg. In 1895, he is elected Scientific Secretary of the Academy with the rank and title of General in the Tsarist civil service. He becomes famous in 1914 for his greatest invention, a condensation isomer of bisphenol A and acetone, now called Dianin's Compound.

Although married, Aleksandr falls in love with Marie Havard, a 26-year-old Frenchwoman living in St. Petersburg. In 1903, they conceive a child. Pavel Aleksandrovich Dianin, the illegitimate issue of this adulterous relationship between a Russian father and a French mother—whose birth was ultimately legitimized by a decree of the Tsar—is my grand-father. He lived with his mother at 6 Kirochnaya Street in the center of St. Petersburg.

☆

In December 1918, Aleksandr Dianin and Marie Havard both succumb, two days apart, to the Spanish influenza. Pavel is 15 years old. He is an orphan. Russia is wracked by famine and the Civil War, which began immediately after the Russian Revolution and lasted from November 1917 to October 1922.

Father Jean Amoudru, a French Catholic priest of the parish of Our Lady of Lourdes in St. Petersburg, saves his life.[9] Since Marie renounced Pavel's French citizenship on his behalf, the boy has no foreign passport and thus, in view of the regime's ban on Soviet citizens travelling abroad, has no right to leave the country. So Father Amoudru intervenes with contacts at the French consulate, which finally grants Pavel a passport that does not bear his actual name—Pavel Aleksandrovich Dianin—but Paul Havard (Paul, which is French for Pavel, and Havard, which is his mother's family name).

Thus, in the course of a few months, Pavel loses his parents, his name and his citizenship, although he continues to use "Pavel." In March 1919, at the age of 16, he leaves his home-land forever.

At the Finnish frontier, Pavel falls into the hands of German soldiers. He is interned in a camp at Terijoki, Finland. Three weeks later, the British military mission charged with disarming German troops in Finland liberates the prisoners and sends them by special train to Turku, where they board a ship for Sweden. After an arduous, month-long journey to France via Sweden, Norway and Britain, Pavel finally arrives in Paris, penniless, alone and very much at the end of his rope.

But Pavel is resourceful, a natural-born entrepreneur. Once settled in the French capital, he studies engineering, paying special attention to the work of the Russian scientist Nikolai Zhukovskiy, founder of aerodynamics. He creates his own business devoted to the design, manufacture and sale of industrial fans.

Pavel is an intense worker. He is tough and persistent. His motto is: "As long as the ball isn't punctured, it bounces back."

He is highly intelligent. He listens a lot and says little. Everyone comes to him for advice.

This man who suffered so much has a hard time smiling, but he is gentle and humble of heart.

I see him again in the last years of his life. He is seated at his desk studying the best chess players of the 20th century in minute detail. What serenity, what patience, what self-control! His entire being exudes an indescribable peace. With him, there are no insurmountable problems, no crisis that cannot be overcome.

☆

In 1926, he marries Nina Anossova who, six years previously, fled Russia with her parents and two sisters.

Nina finds this reserved young man more attractive than all the former officers of the Russian White Army who frequent her parents' flat on rue Molière in hopes of making an impression on Nina and her sisters.

☆

Nina was born on the same day as Pavel—February 28, 1903—in the southern Russian city of Saratov.

She is the descendant of a long line of fervent Old Believers—Orthodox Christians who, refusing to accept the reforms introduced by Patriarch Nikon in 1666, separated from the main body of the Russian church. The state regarded the Old Belief as schismatic and waged a campaign of persecution against it. This caused Nina's ancestors to flee European Russia in the late 17th century. They settled on the banks of the Yenisey River in Siberia and later in Saratov on the Volga River, where they built a fleet of river vessels to transport wheat.

Members of Russia's leading merchants' guild, the Anossovs

7   My great grandfather Aleksandr
    Dianin. St. Petersburg, 1900.

8   My great-grandmother Marie
    Havard. St. Petersburg, 1900.

9   My paternal grandfather,
    Pavel Aleksandrovich Dianin.
    St. Petersburg, 1915.

10  My paternal grandmother,
    Nina Anossova Havard.
    Marseilles, 1921.

carry on the traditions of the Hanseatic merchants of Novgorod. They are patriots, Slavophiles and traditionalists; they are religious believers dedicated to philanthropy. They all bear archaic and biblical names. Nina's grandfather is called Isaiah, her father is named Yefim.

Yefim is very rich. His young wife, Elena Kern, is very beautiful. He marries her for her beauty; she marries him for his money. They have two daughters, Ksenia and Nina, who would become my grandmother. In 1904, after five years of marriage, Elena falls in love with an architect from St. Petersburg who bears the superb name of Alexandre Legrand (in English—Alexander the Great). He is a Frenchman born in Russia. Elena, 23 years of age, divorces her husband and marries Legrand, who is 48. They take up residence in Legrand's house on Vassilevskiy Island in St. Petersburg. Together they will have a daughter, Natasha.

☆

In 1914, the family leaves St. Petersburg and takes up residence in Mariupol, on the Sea of Azov, where Legrand is building a factory to produce electrical cables for military use. Then the Revolution and Civil War break like a tsunami over Russia. After many adventures and a long, dangerous flight across the steppe of Kuban, they set out for Feodosiya in Crimea and arrive six months before the defeat of the White Army.

Alarmed at the prospect of a Bolshevik victory, the family loses no time in moving to Constantinople, then to Marseille and finally to Paris.

☆

From her earliest youth, Nina comes under a variety of influences: Her father, a hard worker, is an Orthodox Christian of the Old Believer tradition; her mother, a frivolous Lutheran, believes only in herself; her step-father, a Catholic, does not believe in anything.

Nina's sister, Ksenia, is admitted at 12 years of age to the

Pavlovskiy Institute, a school for young girls in St. Petersburg under the patronage of the Dowager Empress. Ksenia emerges a convinced Orthodox Christian and monarchist. Her half-sister, Natasha, was baptized Lutheran, like her mother, but later opts for hedonism. As for Nina, who always thirsts for universality, she embarks on a long road that will lead her to Catholicism, which she will embrace without ever renouncing the Orthodox traditions of her youth.

☆

Nina is all sweetness and refined sensibility. If Artschil had a gaze of remarkable intensity, Nina has a voice one does not soon forget: a child's voice emanating from a child's heart. Nina is capable of being surprised and moved by the simplest, most ordinary things.

My grandmother spends her free time reading Chekhov, her favorite writer. When she was a teenager, she dreamed of being a teacher in a village school. Instead, God willed that she would teach me. It was she who gave me the language and culture of her country. It was she who played the most important role in my intellectual formation.

# THE MAGNANIMOUS ONES

Everything about my grandparents was simple, even if they led turbulent lives. My parents, by contrast, are complicated, even if they appear outwardly serene.

They came of age in the post-World War II era, in which it was easier to live physically but harder to live spiritually.

Also, it is easier to be an immigrant than the child of immigrants. The immigrant knows where he comes from: He experiences no identity crisis. The children of immigrants, however, are always prone to such crises; they are forever searching for their roots.

Nevertheless, my parents are fighters. They are determined to get ahead and make their way, and in that they succeed.

☆

My mother, Irene, is the only child of Artschil Gedevanashvili and Madeleine Ducroq. My father, Cyril, is the only child of Paul Havard (Pavel Dianin) and Nina Anossova. My mother was born in 1938, my father in 1929. They met in 1959 at a meeting of Catholic and Orthodox intellectuals at Nina and Pavel's house in Paris. They married several months later. They would have three children: Stéphane, Alexandre and Marie.

11  My mother, Irene Gedevanishvili,
    with my sister, Marie. Pyrenees,
    1967.

12  My father, Kirill Pavlovich
    Dianin-Havard. Brittany, 1980.

13  Brothers: Stéphane Havard (left)
    with the author. Paris, 1980.

☆

If the totality of Artschil's being is concentrated in his gaze, and Nina's personality finds expression in her voice, Irene is defined by her smile. My mother smiles her marvelous smile at everyone she meets, but above all at children, teenagers and students. All who recall her think of her intense and sincere smile. Her smile is her contribution to the human race.

But she is also capable of not smiling in the least. Sometimes she has terrifying moods. She can be judgmental, get angry and annihilate people as quickly, intensely and sincerely as she loves them. If she entertains the slightest doubt about the purity of your intentions, she reduces you to dust without hesitation. But she is capable of saying she is sorry, and of warmly and sincerely embracing the people she has hurt.

☆

My father loves authenticity. He is a rebel and a provocateur. He cannot stand social convention. He takes great pleasure in putting anxious people at ease. He speaks off-the-cuff saying whatever enters his head.

He is an engineer who never worked as an engineer. He is a businessman who has factories around the world, but who dreams of teaching history and philosophy.

☆

My parents have great humanitarian and Christian ideals, but at home Jesus Christ is never spoken of. If someone prays, he or she never does so openly. There is a Christian spirit, but when it comes to the person and the teaching of Christ, we are by and large ignorant. We are Christians in spite of ourselves. I would discover Christianity—the doctrine and dogma, the words and music—later in the unexpected confines of law school, thanks to my encounter with Christians of deep faith studying there. But more of that later.

As part of our education, our father takes us to the theater to see "Crime and Punishment" and "The Portrait of Dorian

Gray." He takes us to the movies to see Andrei Tarkovsky's "The Mirror." He takes us to Egypt and New Orleans. He throws us into the water at the age of three and teaches us to swim against the current. He teaches us to sail on the high seas and not be afraid. We sail through storms on the Atlantic Ocean. He makes us navigate the fjords of Norway.

I have learned more at sea than anywhere else. It is at sea that I have dreamt my wildest dreams.

☆

In raising me and my siblings, my parents make demands and give direction, but the thing that stands out is their respect for our freedom. Only motorbikes and jeans are forbidden. The former are believed to be dangerous, the latter unbecoming (or so we were told.)

We are taught to do what others usually do not do. Our parents love France, but do not consider themselves—indeed, are afraid of becoming—French.

My brother Stéphane is one year older and my sister Marie one year younger. We are good friends and rarely fight among ourselves. We do lots of things together.

☆

My father works very hard, and his firm, which manufactures industrial fans in France, the United States and Japan, is doing well. He inherited it from his father and led its expansion abroad. We live in a comfortable, spacious apartment in one of the most beautiful parts of Paris and spend our summers at our wonderful dacha on Brittany's Atlantic coast.

The Paris apartment, the country house, the sailboat—they are not only for us. They are also for our friends, especially those of more modest means. In the summer, our family grows by three or four as friends come to stay. Each has his or her own space.

☆

Unscrupulous Japanese business interests begin counterfeiting one of my father's main products. He sues them—in vain, as the Japanese courts will not defend the rights and interests of foreigners. The French Minister of Foreign Trade did what she could to resolve the matter and even visited my father's factory in the Shizuoka Prefecture—but to no avail. In 1986, the business goes bankrupt.

My father is at a low ebb, but my mother gets him back on his feet. Life goes on.

☆

In 1991, the Soviet regime falls. A year later, my parents move to Georgia, thus fulfilling my maternal grandfather's most cherished dream—that the family return to liberated Georgia. My mother is 54 years old.

War breaks out between Georgia and the secessionist province of Abkhazia. There are Georgian refugees in need of humanitarian aid in the mountains of the neighboring province of Svaneti. My parents fly there by helicopter. Once there, my mother disappears in the general chaos. My father finds her after nightfall at the airport of Koutaïssi. Her hands and feet are frozen. A doctor massages them. My father is pale with fear for his wife's health. The doctor whispers in his ear, "Her pulse is 27. I have never seen anyone survive with such a low pulse."

Irene Gedevanishvili has heart problems, but she will live for another 20 years. She will serve her country to the end of her days.

She dies on May 26, 2011 (the Georgian national holiday) in the Caucasian foothills of Kakheti—a small, mountainous province in eastern Georgia—not far from the Bodbe monastery, which has contained Saint Nino's relics since 347 AD. The funeral Mass is celebrated in Georgian by a Polish priest in the Holy Mother of God Church of Bethlehem in Tbilisi. The burial rite is celebrated in Russian by a Spanish priest who is the regional vicar of Opus Dei in Russia, accompanied by a Georgian Orthodox choir. A liturgy for the deceased is celebrated several days later in Paris by the rector of the Georgian parish church of Saint Nino, but because the church building is too small, it is held in the Greek Orthodox cathedral.

When I think of my late mother, I often picture her dressed in a long gown of burgundy velvet, a black belt around her waist and, around her neck, an impressive gold medal of Saint George slaying the dragon.

My father retraces his roots in Russia. His father, Paul Havard (Pavel Dianin), had a half-brother named Sergei Dianin. Whereas Pavel was born of Aleksandr Dianin and his mistress, Marie Havard, Sergei was the son of Aleksandr and his wife, Borodin's adopted daughter, Elizabeth. Pavel and Sergei met for the first time at their father's funeral in December 1918. After Pavel emigrated to France, they exchanged letters several times. But as the new regime considered contact with foreigners an anti-Soviet provocation, Pavel ceased all correspondence with Sergei so as not to compromise him. The family heard nothing more from or about Sergei after 1923.

In 2000, I begin my search for evidence of Sergei. On the Internet, I come across this: "Sergei Aleksandrovich Dianin, Saint Petersburg 1888, Davydovo 1968, Soviet musician and mathematician, son of the chemist A. Dianin and E. Borodin, adopted daughter of the composer. Author of a biography of Aleksandr Borodin (Moscow, 1955), which was translated into English (Oxford, 1963)."

Also on the Internet, I find another Sergei Dianin: born in 1965 in Moscow, graduate of the Moscow Institute of Aeronautics (1988) and the CEO of the Rolf Leasing company. I write to the institute, which forwards my letter to Sergei. He responds immediately. We meet in Moscow. We could not determine if we are related. I am impressed by Sergei. He is an engaging, energetic guy. It would be great if we are related. In any case, Sergei becomes a friend and agrees to help me in my search.

My father and I learn that during the Second World War, Sergei (my father's half-uncle) moved with his wife and son to the family seat of Davydovo, where he lived until his death in 1968; that his son died of tuberculosis in 1943; that we are, therefore, the sole descendants of Aleksandr Dianin, the chemist; and that, in 1980, the Dianin family residence became the Aleksandr Borodin Museum, the only museum in the world dedicated to the Russian composer.

In 2005, I drive to Davydovo with Sergei and his wife, Natasha. The director of the Borodin museum is bowled over to meet a direct descendant of Aleksandr Dianin. He knew nothing of the existence of my grandfather, Paul Havard (Dianin). So as not to land in trouble with the regime, Sergei never told anyone in Davydovo he had a half-brother living in France.

In the museum, there are two large rooms, one of which is devoted to Borodin, the other to the Dianin family. The latter is dominated by a portrait of Pavel Afanasevich Dianin, our common ancestor and the village's first vicar. The room is also graced by a photograph of my grandfather, Pavel Aleksandrovich, and my father, Kirill Pavlovich.

At Davydovo, life goes on. It centers around the imposing Church of the Transfiguration, which the Bolsheviks, by the grace of God, did not destroy.

# THE MARTYRS

It is 1975 and I am 13 years old. In the West, we are experiencing the "crisis of the Church." Christianity is being subverted by some priests, bishops and cardinals who have lost the Faith but who, inspired by the Devil, remain in the Church so as to destroy her from within.

At school, a teacher determined to preserve our Christian identity invites a group of experts to talk to us about the persecution of religion in the USSR. They show us slides of dynamited churches reduced to rubble. They show us photos of psychiatric wards where Christians who persist in their faith are "cured." They show us pictures of martyrs—Orthodox, Catholic and Protestant—tortured for their fidelity to the Gospel.

During recess, I retreat to a corner of the schoolyard rather than play soccer with my friends. I feel that someone or something is about to take possession of my soul. I am no longer the same. I experience great sorrow and great joy. It is the Holy Spirit waking me up, taking me by the hand, taking over my heart—even though I know nothing at all about the Holy Spirit.

The martyrs enter my heart like an arrow piercing the body.

☆

In a Western world wrecked by materialism, the desire for an easy life and the insatiable thirst for gratification, the martyrs will be my salvation. Christianity for me is not the decomposing corpse of the West, which I encounter everywhere. Christianity is the all-victorious Cross, raised up from the Golgotha of the 20th century. It is the bright, red blood of faithfulness, mercy and love of God—the blood of the martyrs.

My Christian education to this point is limited to the basics. At home, we do not speak of God. At school, the teachers do but have no idea what they are talking about. There is no basic formation, no catechism, no moral teaching. No one speaks of the Ten Commandments. No one ever speaks of the virtues. I know there are three important things called faith, hope and charity, but what our teachers say about them amounts to little more than ideologically inspired psychobabble. It bears no relationship to anything Christ taught.

The martyrs are, for me, the only ones qualified to bear witness to the Faith. I look to them and only to them. I feel their presence and their support everywhere.

## THE RUSSIAN IDEA

For me, school is hell. Despite my best efforts, I am invari-
ably next-to-last in my class. Only in swimming am I any
good—I am the first in my class.

I study English, but I am not allowed to take German as a
second language. They insist I take Spanish instead because,
in their words, "Spanish is for idiots!" My mother, who
was once a Spanish teacher, has a fit. She dashes off to the
school: "My son will study German; I can teach him Spanish
myself." She wins the battle. I study German.

I am bad at Latin. No one even tries to pronounce it
correctly on the pretext that no one knows how it was originally pronounced. As punishment, in place of Latin, they
make me study technology. This time my mother does not
go on the warpath.

☆

My parents are concerned for my future. I like to prune
trees and cut the grass, so they think I will be a gardener.

☆

One day, I ask my grandmother Nina to read me something in Russian. She smiles and chooses a story by Chekhov

called "The Student." In summary:

> It is Good Friday. It is cold and night is falling as a young student of the clerical academy, the son of a sacristan, is returning home from the hunt. Passing along the river past a desolate village, he is drawn by the light of a fire in a garden. He stops to warm himself. The fire is tended by a widow and her daughter. He tells them of the events that took place in the court of the high priest when Jesus was arrested and, above all, of Peter's denial of the Master. The widow is moved to tears; her daughter seems pained. The student thinks the widow is sobbing so freely because "all that happened to Peter before the Crucifixion must have some relation to her." Clearly, what he had related to the widow, "which had happened nineteen centuries ago, had a relation to the present—to both women, to the desolate village, to himself, to all people."

> Then he sets out on the road again, only to halt when this thought occurs to him: "The past is linked with the present by an unbroken chain of events flowing one out of another." And the narrator notes: "It seemed to him that he had just seen both ends of that chain; that when he touched one end the other quivered." The narrator describes the landscape of early spring, the thaw and the "mysterious happiness," which "took possession of him little by little, and life seemed to him enchanting, marvelous and full of lofty meaning."[10]

There is no action, no intrigue, but in the four pages of this story, Chekhov gives us all the beauty and truth of which he was capable.

As my grandmother reads, I understand nothing, but I am captivated by her high emotion and decide then and there to learn Russian. She will be my teacher.

☆

The Russian language liberates my spirit. I begin to take an interest in reading. I read the works that interest me, works very different from the ones we are required to read in school.

What strikes me about Russian literature is its moral and Christian content. It is aimed at the reader's heart. It seeks to ennoble and transform.

A new world opens before my eyes so different from the Cartesian ("I think therefore I am") society in which I am being raised. In this new world, there is much more to being than mere thinking.

☆

I read Chekhov who seems "immoral" because he presents facts objectively without ever taking a moral stand (or so it seems). But my grandmother helps me see that behind his apparent neutrality lies a fierce condemnation of nostalgia and melancholy. These can be excellent qualities in strong-willed persons but are great faults in people of weaker character. Chekhov demands emotional sincerity, which he insists should be reflected in our actions.

I read Dostoevsky who opens my eyes to worldly realities, to the devils all around us, to the war taking place in heaven as on earth, and to the contradictions in and the drama of atheistic humanism. I understand that where Christ is concerned, indifference is not an option—either you are for Him or against Him.

I read Tolstoy. I am moved by his struggle against the social passivity of so many Christians. Tolstoy expands my mind. The danger does not come from external sources— from Christianity's declared enemies—but from inside, from a Christianity that is neither the salt of the earth nor the light of the world. I understand that atheistic humanism is the fruit not only of deviant philosophical thought, but also of the absence of an authentic Christian humanism.

☆

I discover something that completely surprises me: "The Russian Idea."

Russians seek to define themselves as a people in order to come to grips with their own collective essence and discern God's eternal plan for their nation. Russians believe they have an important mission to accomplish in Europe and the world. They are interested, above all, in the philosophy of history.

I read Pyotr Chaadaev (1794-1856): "There are great peoples, just as there are great historic personalities, which one cannot explain by the natural laws of the intelligence, peoples who are mysteriously guided by the supreme logic of Providence. Such is our people. ... I have the profound conviction that our vocation is to find an answer to the important questions that concern humanity."[11] And: "The day will come when we will be the intellectual center of Europe."[12]

I read Vladimir Soloviev (1853-1900): "The face of the slave, which is the face of our nation these days, the sad situation of Russia economically and otherwise, none of that undermines its vocation, but, on the contrary, confirms it. For the supreme force which the Russian people are called to inject into humanity is a force which is not of this world. Order and material richness do not count for anything here."[13]

I read Nikolai Berdyaev (1874-1948): "Western culture is a culture of progress. ... The Russian people, meanwhile, are a *people of the end*,"[14] that is, an eschatological people created and prepared by God to fulfill a very specific mission at the end of history.

☆

Chaadaev, Soloviev and Berdyaev—because they are Christians—hate all manifestations of nationalism and provincialism. They are thinkers and true patriots because they love their homeland in truth, without feeling any need to humiliate other nations or deny the often dramatic reality of their history. "Love of the homeland is a beautiful thing," writes Chaadaev, "but even more beautiful is love of the truth. ... It is not the homeland but truth that leads to heaven. ... I did not learn to love my country with eyes closed, head bowed and mouth shut. ... I find that a man can be useful to his country only if he sees it clearly."[15]

Chadaaev, Soloviev and Berdyaev had a profound impact on my evolving worldview.

The Russian idea seems to be confirmed by the prophetic words of the Virgin Mary, the Queen of Peace, in one of her apparitions in October 1981 in Medjugorje, Bosnia: "The Russian people will be the people who glorify God the most. The West has made civilization progress, but without God—as if they were their own creators."[16]

I spend long days with my grandmother, Nina. She tells me surprising things about her youth in St. Petersburg, about Russia, about her family's flight during the Civil War and about my grandfather Pavel, who never said anything about his past. Only Nina, his devoted wife, knows the whole story.

# VOCATION

M y grandmother, Nina, always had a strong devotion to Saint Michael. When I was born, she insisted that my parents name me not just Alexandre—in honor of Aleksandr Dianin—but also Michael, after the Archangel. So I became Michel Alexandre.

For my 15th birthday, my grandmother gives me an icon of Saint Michael, the Supreme Commander of the Heavenly Hosts, which she commissioned from a Russian iconographer. I hang it over my bed.

Nina soon becomes convinced that I need more than one Michael to protect me: For my 16th birthday, she gives me an image depicting Michael as the *Archistrategos*—the Supreme Commander of the Angelic Legions. With his armor and sword, Michael looks like a samurai. My eyes meet his gaze every time I leave my room.

☆

It is 1979 and I am 17 years old. In a few months, I will graduate from secondary school.

I must decide on a career but am more concerned about what kind of life I will lead, what kind of man I will be. I know

14  *Icon of Our Lady of Fatima.*

that if I do not decide the matter soon, others will do it for me—my parents, my friends, the girls I know, French society with its empty slogans and fads.

In childhood and adolescence, I often dreamt and entertained lots of hopes. I had a certain notion of what my life should be.

Everyone keeps advising me to study hard, work for my father's company, make plenty of money and marry a beautiful girl.

I am stricken with anxiety. I am profoundly sad. It is the most sorrowful year of my life.

I speak to my parents about it. They think it is a crisis of adolescence. I can hardly blame them.

I go my own way.

I seek refuge at the famous Sacré Coeur Basilica at the summit of the Montmartre butte. Sacré Coeur is French for the Sacred Heart of Jesus, in which I now find comfort and consolation.

☆

I finish secondary school. My parents offer to pay for a trip abroad. I choose the Holy Land.

I go there in search of light. In the desert between Jerusalem and Jericho, I find it.

It is an unexpected light that says, "Trust in me."

My journey ends on the Red Sea—windsurfing.

☆

In the fall of 1980, I begin studying law at L'Université Paris Descartes. There are 300 students in my class. I make several new friends. I enroll in a club devoted to French boxing,[17] which my brother Stéphane, a medical student, has been frequenting for several years.

☆

When my grandfather Pavel dies, I move in with my grandmother Nina. In the morning, I study law at the University; in the evening, I practice Russian with my grandmother.

In the small garden, there is a birch tree that my grand-father planted years ago. In summer, I set up a desk in the shade of its branches.

☆

One day in April 1981, I am seated in an amphitheater-style classroom waiting for a lecture on criminal law to begin. The packed room is abuzz with chatter. An announcement is made that the professor will be half an hour late.

So I open a book I just bought from a *bouquiniste*[18] near Notre Dame Cathedral in Paris. Richard Wurmbrand is a Romanian writer of Jewish origin. Although originally a Marxist, he converted to Christianity in 1938 at 29 years of age. In 1945, he became a Lutheran pastor in Bucharest where he spread the Gospel among Soviet Red Army soldiers. In 1948, he was arrested by the Communists and condemned to 20 years in prison. In 1964, Norwegian Protestants arranged for his departure from Romania. He took up residence in the United States and spent the rest of his life defending Christians who were being persecuted for their faith in Communist and Moslem countries.[19]

I love Wurmbrand's books. Although the Communists tortured him brutally for 14 years, he loved his enemies. He prayed for them and their conversion. There is no bitterness in his writing. There is only the joy of one who has suffered for Christ. Wurmbrand was a friend of Russia: "For me, to preach the Gospel to the Russians is heaven on earth. I have preached the Gospel to men of many nations, but I have never seen a people drink in the Gospel like the Russians."[20]

No sooner do I open one of Wurmbrand's books testifying to the power of grace and its triumph over evil, than a student approaches and asks what I am reading. We talk briefly. His name is Maxime. We quickly become good friends.

We study together.

Maxime has two great passions in life: Bruce Lee of kung-fu movie fame and the Virgin Mary. Often after class, we go either to the movies to see Bruce Lee or to Notre Dame Cathedral to visit the Mother of God.

Maxime teaches me to meditate every day on the Gospel and talk to God like a son talks to his father. Every month, he takes me to visit those whom he calls "the poor of the Virgin"—old people who have been virtually abandoned.

☆

One day, Maxime invites me to an Opus Dei center near avenue Mozart. He introduces me to Xavier, the center's director. Xavier is 20 years our senior. As a professor of history at the Sorbonne, he is recognized internationally as an expert on the Mexican Revolution.

Xavier tells me about Josemaria Escriva, the founder of Opus Dei, and his teaching: the search for Christ in ordinary life—at work, at home and in society. The world is not an obstacle to Christian life. On the contrary, it is in and through the world that we discover Christ and enter into unity with Him.

Opus Dei aims to divinize ordinary life. It is the fullness of divine filiation in the middle of the world. I can remain where I am and continue to do what I do while giving my actions an entirely new meaning.

Holiness for everyone—that is a deeply evangelical thing. Holiness as a life ideal. Such a thing had never occurred to me. And yet it seems like such a logical and natural goal for a Christian.

☆

I feel very much at home at this Opus Dei center. I meet students from many other schools and universities in Paris. They speak about things big and small in a very natural way. I spend hours every week there studying in the library.

A priest lives there. I speak to him often. He asks me if I am studying hard, if every day I devote time to meditating on the Gospel and talking to God, if I try to bring people I meet closer to God. It is not the third degree but spiritual direction, in which the priest gives practical advice on how to achieve sanctity, pray and examine one's conscience.

☆

On May 13, 1981, Pope John Paul II is shot in broad daylight. His condition is critical.

It is the first time that I pray for a pope. Previously, I did not know who he was, nor did I care.

The assassination attempt occurs on the anniversary of Mary's first apparition at Fatima, Portugal, in 1917. At Fatima she spoke of Russia and the pope.

I could not imagine then that John Paul II would play a very important role in my life.

☆

It is December 1982. A year and half has passed since my first encounter with Opus Dei and the attack on John Paul II. I progress in my studies and in my interior life.

Duccio, whose real name is Francesco, is a professor of Italian at the Sorbonne with whom I have been speaking about my spiritual life for some time. He asks me to think seriously about vocation. Duccio thinks I am mature enough to make a decision that will entail a lifetime commitment. He thinks Opus Dei is my way. He speaks of these things as we are approaching the Chapel of Our Lady of the Miraculous Medal on rue du Bac.

We enter the chapel that was built on the site of the apparition of Our Lady to Saint Catherine Labouré in 1830. Our Lady appeared with the world at her feet, crushing a serpent under foot and wearing rings of different colors that projected rays of light over the globe. Our Lady said, "The rays of light represent the graces I confer on people who ask for them. The rings that do not project light represent the graces I did not confer because no one asked for them." Around the Virgin, Catherine made out the words: "O Mary, conceived without sin, pray for those who have recourse to thee." Then the image rotated and Catherine saw a large "M," Mary's initial, surmounted by a cross. Beneath it, there were two hearts—

that of Jesus crowned with thorns and that of Mary pierced by a sword. Twelve stars surrounded the image.

☆

Before Duccio spoke to me about vocation, I was already planning a trip to Fatima with Olivier, a friend since childhood. Olivier was last in our class and I was next to last.[21]

On December 26, we leave for Portugal. We get off at Estremoz and walk and hitchhike for a week until we arrive in Lisbon and then in Fatima. We sleep in tents along the way.

☆

Fatima. From May 13 to October 13, 1917, Our Lady appeared on six occasions to three children aged seven to ten—Lucia, Jacinta and Francisco. All three came from poor peasant families.

On July 13, the Blessed Virgin showed them hell and said:

> "You have seen hell where the souls of poor sinners go. To save them, God wishes to establish in the world devotion to my Immaculate Heart. If what I say to you is done, many souls will be saved and there will be peace. The war is going to end:[22] but if people do not cease offending God, a worse one will break out during the Pontificate of Pius XI. When you see the night sky illuminated by an unknown light, know that this is the great sign given you by God that he is about to punish the world for its crimes, by means of war, famine, and persecutions of the Church and of the Holy Father. To prevent this, I shall come to ask for the consecration of Russia to my Immaculate Heart and the Communion of reparation on First Saturdays. If my requests are heeded, Russia will be converted, and there will be peace; if not, she will spread her errors throughout the world, causing wars and persecutions of the Church. The good will be martyred; the Holy Father will have much to suffer; various nations will be annihilated. In

the end, my Immaculate Heart will triumph. The Holy Father will consecrate Russia to me, and she shall be converted, and a period of peace will be granted to the world."[23]

Lucia recounted further:

"We saw an angel with a flaming sword in his left hand; flashing, it gave out flames that looked as though they would set the world on fire; but they died out in contact with the splendor that Our Lady radiated towards him from her right hand: pointing to the earth with his right hand, the Angel cried out in a loud voice: 'penance, penance, penance!' And we saw in an immense light that is God—'something similar to how people appear in a mirror when they pass in front of it'—a bishop dressed in white. We had the impression that it was the Holy Father. Other bishops, priests, men and women religious going up a steep mountain, at the top of which there was a big cross of rough-hewn trunks as of a cork-tree with the bark; before reaching there the Holy Father passed through a large city half in ruins. Trembling and with halting step, afflicted with pain and sorrow, he prayed for the souls of the corpses he met on his way; having reached the top of the mountain, on his knees at the foot of the cross he was killed by a group of soldiers who fired bullets and arrows at him, and in the same way there died one after another the other bishops, priests, men and women religious, and various lay people of different ranks and positions. Beneath the two arms of the cross there were two angels each with a crystal aspersorium in his hand, in which they gathered up the blood of the martyrs, and, with it, sprinkled the souls that were making their way to God."[24]

☆

The blood of the martyrs purifies and nourishes the souls of those who make their way to God. ...

This has been my trajectory since that day at school in 1975, when I was 13 and they showed us slides depicting the persecution of Christians in the Soviet Union, at which point the martyrs entered my life—like an arrow piercing the heart.

☆

The prophecy of July 13, 1917 at Fatima took place three days before the first Bolshevik attempt to seize power. The last apparition occurred on October 13, 1917, just three weeks before the Bolsheviks finally succeeded in pulling off their *coup d'etat.*

That year, the Virgin said she would ask, at the appropriate time, that Russia be consecrated to her Immaculate Heart. That time came in 1929 when she asked Pope Pius XI, through Lucia's intervention, to carry out this consecration.

But the Virgin's request went unheeded.

It was the year of Stalin's Great Break that unleashed the whirlwind of forced industrialization.

Rivers of blood flowed in Russia. They exterminated peasants by the millions.

☆

In 1936, Lucia asked Jesus why he would not save Russia without the Holy Father consecrating the nation to His mother's Immaculate Heart.

"Because," said Jesus, "I want all of my Church to recognize this consecration as a triumph for the Immaculate Heart of Mary, so as to extend its cult, and to place, alongside devotion to my Divine Heart, devotion to her Immaculate Heart."

"But dear God," responded Lucia, "the Holy Father will not believe me if you do not move him yourself by a special inspiration."

"The Holy Father!" Jesus replied, "Pray a lot for the Holy Father. He will make this consecration, but it will be late. Meanwhile, the Immaculate Heart of Mary will save Russia, which is entrusted to her."[25]

☆

"It will be late!" The tragic destiny of tens of millions of human lives passed before our eyes. "That will come later!" Christ spoke these words with infinite sorrow.

☆

Fatima shed light on the most dramatic events of the 20th century. It revealed the intimate link of the Mother of God to the Russian people!

☆

I join Opus Dei in January 1983 in Fatima, Portugal.

I am 20 years old, a third-year law student … and a member of Opus Dei—the Work of God. I did not choose the Work of God, God chose me with all my defects and qualities, such as they were.

☆

My vocation is a call to be, think and act in a *particular* way. It is the criterion by which I measure all my actions, and the principle that gives unity to my entire life.

My vocation is not my mission. My mission is the *specific thing* I must do, my contribution to humanity. I do not know my mission. I must discover it. I will discover it when I realize what I am good at. I will know that later.

☆

I let myself be changed, be formed. That is what I do during the first years of my vocation.

But what I am, the substance of my own being, only grows stronger with each passing day. I become more and more who I am.

☆

Several months after I join Opus Dei, my brother, Stéphane, marries a Thai woman named Waurapun. They met as students at North Carolina State University in Raleigh. Stéphane would serve for 20 years as a doctor at the American

Hospital of Paris. He and his wife would have three children: Maxime, Marine and Alice.

My sister, Marie, marries Gilles, a graduate of L'École polytechnique in Paris. Together they fight poverty in the slums on the outskirts of Paris. Later, Gilles becomes the comptroller at Peugeot Citroën. Marie and Gilles would have six children together: Nadiéjda, Laélia, Pierre-Cyril, Tinatine, Amandine and Marcelin.

☆

The great majority of members of Opus Dei are married. That stands to reason since most people on earth are called to marry and find God in marriage.

The women who are so important in my life—my mother and sister—are paragons of femininity. The girls I know and date are wonderful, but I am not thinking about marriage. I am also not thinking about celibacy. I am thinking only about Russia.

After Fatima, I know that marriage is out of the question. I am embarked on a different path—to make a total gift of myself to God without any intermediary or intermediation, including the intermediation of human love. This is an adventure that will last my entire life, yielding fruits of unlimited spiritual fatherhood.

☆

My parents are aware of one thing: What they thought, three years ago, was a crisis of adolescence, was nothing of the kind, but rather a stable and permanent state of being, a positive affirmation of my personality.

They are terrified. They launch a war against me, but this is good for me: It forces me to define myself; it confirms the seriousness and sincerity of my way. In any case, the war will not last long because my father, having just criticized what he called the "folly" of my choice, suddenly speaks words that only increased my admiration for him: "You are free to do what you want!"

Several years later, after I left France, my mother sends me a letter containing this phrase, which moves me deeply: "I know that you have made the right choice, my son."

Clearly, it is not I who makes the choice, but God.

# TBILISI

It is June 1983. I have finished my third year of law school. The moment has come to make my first steps—physically—towards Russia and Georgia. I decide to spend the month of August with my great-aunt, Elena, and her son, Thamaz. The Soviet Embassy grants me a visa.

Elena is the sister of my maternal grandfather Artschil. She was 18 years old in 1927 when her brother fled the Soviet Union. Her husband was shot to death in 1937. It was not until 1967 that she was allowed to leave the USSR for a few months to visit Artschil in Paris. Forty years have elapsed since they last saw each other.

☆

On August 3, 1983, I set foot on Russian soil for the first time. My flight from Paris lands at Moscow's Sheremetevo Airport at three o'clock in the afternoon.

At the time, Yuriy Andropov is the General Secretary of the Communist Party and President of the USSR. Andropov is widely believed to have orchestrated the plot to assassinate Pope John Paul II on May 13, 1981, when he was the head of the KGB.

Many people are praying for me at this hour. They know I have two suitcases—one containing only clothing and the other containing only religious literature, the circulation of which is banned in the USSR. I am carrying Russian-language editions of the Bible and various spiritual writings, which I acquired from the Brussels publishing house Zhizn' s Bogom, which was founded in 1945 by Irina Posnova, the daughter of the noted Russian historian Mikhail Posnov.

For a very tense 30 minutes, a divine spectacle unfolds before my eyes as an officer of the KGB inspects slowly, calmly and precisely the suitcase containing only clothing.

"Is that all you have?" he asks. He is wearing sunglasses, so I cannot tell what he is looking at. At my feet is the other suitcase full of the New Testament in Russian, as plainly visible as the one he just inspected.

"Yes, that's all," I reply.

As I close the suitcase full of clothing, I see he is already examining the belongings of the next passenger.

He doesn't see my second suitcase. He is blinded by my guardian angel.

☆

My cousin Guram and his son, Sandro, who is my age, are traveling 1,020 miles from the Georgian capital of Tbilisi to Moscow to meet me at the airport. Tomorrow, we leave for Tbilisi.

I spend my first night in Moscow at the home of Guram's friends.

I think of my grandmother Nina, of the last night she spent on Russian soil in the spring of 1920 in the port city of Feodosiya in Crimea. She was 17 years old. She wanted to remain in Russia, but her stepfather was opposed. Terrified by the idea of leaving her country, dissolved in tears, her throat constricted, her heart so heavy she had trouble breathing, her soul cried out to God. It seemed to her that her cry resonated to the ends of the earth. It was Father Vassily, her catechism teacher at Mariupol, who had taught her to pray in this way just months before he was arrested, tortured and shot to death by the Red Guards.

All of that happened 63 years ago. Now, Nina, an old lady, is sitting in her apartment in Paris. She knows I am in Russia. She cannot sleep. She prays.

On the other side of the Caucasus, at Tbilisi, the thoughts of another elderly lady also turn to heaven. It is Elena, my great-aunt. I am the first member of our family to visit Georgia since her brother fled the country in 1927.

☆

Her son, Thamaz, meets me at Tbilisi airport since Guram and Sandro took another plane and will arrive later.

Thamaz is 60 years old. He was 10 when they killed his father. He believes neither in God, nor in man, nor in himself. He never married. His mental and moral universe was formed by those who shot his father.

We approach the house in Red Partisans Street where he and his mother live. He gets out of the car and calls her from a phone booth to say we will soon be at the door of the apartment.

We walk up the staircase very slowly. We are at the front door. The door is ajar and Thamaz pushes it open.

Elena stands there stock-still. She has been expecting me for half a century.

☆

The day after my arrival in Tbilisi, my cousin Sandro, an architecture student, accompanies me to the entrance of Saints Peter and Paul Catholic Church.

"Alex," he says, "if they see me in the church, they'll throw me out of the university. Go in by yourself. I'll wait for you in the car."

I enter the church. I go to the sacristy and introduce myself to Father Johan, the pastor. I put the suitcase full of religious literature on the table.

"Father, here is a gift from your friends in Paris."

He opens the suitcase and cannot believe his eyes. He bursts into tears. He asks me how I got this treasure into Tbilisi. I tell him the story of the miracle of clearing customs.

"I will celebrate Mass for you," he says, "and for those who produced these books."

I attend Mass. At the moment of Holy Communion, I get up and approach the altar. A young man comes up to me and asks if I have been to confession. He has never seen me in church before, and he is horrified by the idea that I might be committing a sacrilege by receiving the Body of Christ while in a state of sin.

Several days later, Sandro and I decide to spend the weekend at Batumi on the Black Sea. On the night of our arrival, we cannot sleep because in a nearby cemetery an old woman is wailing over the tomb of her son. We go out onto the balcony and sit there until the wee hours of the morning talking about life, death and eternity.

# ESCRIVA

Back in Tbilisi, Thamaz lets me have his room. It has a balcony overlooking Red Partisans Street.

I pray on this balcony each morning. I address myself to Saint Josemaria Escriva.

Escriva speaks to me of the future—of a future to be built on the blood of the martyrs.

He whispers inspiring words in my ear: "Do not let your life be barren. Be useful. Make yourself felt. Shine forth with the torch of your faith and your love. With your apostolic life, wipe out the trail of filth and slime left by the corrupt sowers of hatred. And set aflame all the ways of the earth with the fire of Christ that you bear in your heart."[26]

☆

It is 1983. There is no reason to believe communism will be coming to an end anytime soon.

Yesterday, I had to appear at the immigration service. The interrogation room was dominated by the portraits of three devils: Lenin, Ordzhonikidze[27] and Andropov.

☆

It was the absence of Christ from political, social, profes-sional and family life that led to the catastrophe of Bolshevism.

We are all responsible for this. We think that sanctity in the middle of the world is an impossible dream. We think that the achievement of Christian perfection through ordinary activ-ities is an illusion. By entertaining such notions, we wind up leading lives of astounding moral and spiritual mediocrity.

We are indifferent to Christ when he says: "Be perfect as your heavenly Father is perfect."

As a consequence, we distort Christianity to such an extent that its enemies seem more reasonable, attractive and right than Christ's followers.

☆

To seek sanctity in ordinary life—in the barracks, at the university, in the factory, in the studio, in the fields, at home. To sanctify your work, to sanctify yourself through your work, to sanctify others by your work. To put Christ at the summit of all human activities. To convert the prose of each day into heroic verse.

These phrases come from the pen of Escriva. The message, as he was fond of saying, is as old and as new as the Gospel. We have completely forgotten this message and we are paying the price.

☆

I think of Saint Nino. She understood, lived and transmitted this message. Why have we betrayed Nino? Why have we betrayed Christ? Isn't the essence of Christianity the diviniza-tion of man and the transfiguration, by the grace of God, of all earthly realities?

One of the most important Russian theologians of the emigration, Alexander Schmemann, says that the Christian's on-going flight from the world stems from an inability to square the circle of a basic Christian paradox: to be "in the world" but "not of this world."

But if Schmemann is right, why should the failure of some

*15 Icon of Saint Josemaria Escriva de Balaguer*

mean the failure of all? And how to explain the triumph of the first Christians in the world? Although Christianity's foundational ethos has been weakened, can it not be restored? Why have we ceased to believe in the power of grace, in the power of God to act in the middle of the world?

An icon of Saint Josemaria by Muscovite iconographer Aleksandr Sokolov renders Escriva as a giant (literally)—his head is in heaven in the presence of the angels and archangels, the Mother of God and the Infant Jesus, *while his feet remain solidly planted on earth*. This icon symbolizes the strength of God's grace present at the heart of all noble, human activities. It depicts the world, which Escriva loved so passionately: farmers planting seeds, a shepherd leading his sheep out to pasture, fishermen hauling their nets into their boat, a mother teaching her child how to live and how to be. This is the world of Escriva. It is the world of ordinary, everyday life transfigured by the grace of God.

In this icon, the figures, although clearly delineated, are so small and numerous they are hard to see unless viewed at close range. This suggests Escriva's belief that work done for the love of God and in the service of others—work often hidden from everyone but God—is of eternal value.

Escriva's message is capable of transforming the world and restoring Christianity's original impulse.

God communicated this message to him in the form of a vision of Opus Dei—which did not yet exist—on October 2, 1928 in Madrid. This happened even as Stalin was preparing to launch his "Great Experiment," the construction of socialism, that would take tens of millions of lives.

Stalin—you walked through the streets of Tbilisi just under my balcony! You studied in this city's seminary, a seminary where you should have met God. Instead you met the Devil.

☆

On a streetcar in Madrid in the autumn of 1931, the 29-year-old Josemaria Escriva is reading a newspaper. Spain is on the verge of civil war. He feels helpless, incapable of achieving the great task, the urgent mission God gave him three years previously—the founding of Opus Dei.

Suddenly, the Holy Spirit takes hold of his soul and makes him feel an ineffable joy in the deepest part of his being, the joy of divine filiation. Prompted by the Spirit, he starts to shout in a loud voice the words from Scripture: "Abba! Father! Abba."

His fellow passengers take him for a lunatic. He gets off at the next stop and walks for several hours through the streets of Madrid. So immense is the joy communicated to him by the Spirit, he is unable to regain his composure.

☆

Escriva's understanding of humility is entirely revolutionary. For him, humility has less to do with being modest and unassuming than with manifesting the superiority complex of a son or daughter of God and with living accordingly without reservation.

Escriva's works were translated into Russian by Natalia Trauberg, who is widely recognized in her country for translating Ionesco, Chesterton, C. S. Lewis and García Lorca. She is a Russian philologist of Jewish origin and the daughter of the eminent stage director Leonid Trauberg. She was baptized in the Orthodox Church in Soviet times. She calls herself a "wild creature and a half-Catholic." What she likes about Escriva, she says, is the tension in his teaching between humility and magnanimity, between contemplation and action, between the love that pardons and the love that demands. She is struck by his dynamic understanding of humility—a humility appropriate to those who seek God in ordinary life.

☆

With Escriva, all virtues acquire a new meaning. More to the point, they regain their original meaning: They are the virtues of men and women who are immersed in worldly affairs, because they know this is where they will encounter the face of God their Father.

Poverty as a virtue is not the rejection of material possessions; it is the heart's detachment from them. Chastity is not the absence of sex; it is the unique, unconditional and definitive gift of oneself to another. Justice is not (only) the impulse to reform society; it is also the perfect fulfillment of our professional, familial and social obligations. Courage is not just bravery in the face of adversity. It is fidelity, renewed each day, to the path one has chosen.

☆

Escriva preaches the paternity of God with such conviction that He makes him the father of thousands of people on this earth.

"In Escriva, I have found fatherhood," says Tatiana Goricheva, the Russian Orthodox philosopher and writer who was expelled from the USSR in 1980 for her "Christian feminism."

☆

Escriva suffers as no one should have to suffer. He witnesses the death of his three younger sisters while still a child, and he is sorely tempted to rebel against God. He lives in absolute poverty. He suffers the horrors of the Spanish Civil War, including persecution for his religious beliefs. He suffers severe, life-threatening illness. He suffers for the crises wracking the Church.

Escriva suffers as the prophets suffered—he suffers calumny; he is in the trash bin of humanity. All of the emasculated on earth get together and decide to destroy this exponent of Christian virility, who dares to preach the universal call to holiness without asking their permission.

But Escriva is happy, unspeakably happy: "God is my Father, even if he allows me to suffer. He loves me tenderly, even as he wounds me. ... Suffering is the surest sign of my filiation, because he treats me like his Divine Son."[28]

48

# Wojtyla & Soloviev

In 1983, I begin to take an interest in the teaching and activities of Pope John Paul II.

John Paul II loves Russia. He has read Chadaaev, Soloviev and Berdyaev.

☆

It is this Marian pope who, on March 25, 1984, makes the consecration requested by our Blessed Mother at Fatima, in communion with the bishops worldwide. This consecration deals above all with Russia.

It is this Slav pope who, in 1985, writes an encyclical honoring Saints Cyril and Methodius, the apostles of the Slavs and fathers of East Slavic culture. This pope's vision of Europe is more judicious and universal than that of his predecessors.

In 1988, he publishes an important apostolic letter on the occasion of the millennium of the baptism of Russia. Reading this letter, one grasps the extent to which the Polish pope loves and understands Russia.

Wojtyla's "Russian doctrine" can be summarized in three points:

1. The greatness of Russia, her specific contribution to the spiritual well-being of humanity, is linked to the Byzantine-Slav cultural and religious tradition, whose foundations were laid by Cyril and Methodius in the 9th century. To Latinize Russia would be to render her sterile. This would condemn the universal Church to a morbid provincialism and impede the achievement of Christian unity.

2. The Church, by tradition, comprises two great cultural forms—Eastern and Western—that complement each other like two lungs in the same organism. Western culture is more logical and rational; Eastern culture is more mystical and intuitive. "The world has always been divided into two parts—the East and the West," writes Piotr Chadaaev, whom John Paul II studied in detail. "In the East, the human spirit is formed by concentrating on itself, by being enclosed in itself. In the West, it is developed by leaving itself, by surging forth from all sides, overcoming all exterior obstacles."[29]

   Western culture is more masculine, Eastern culture more feminine. This natural complementarity should engender love, not confrontation. Cultural and religious nationalism, the rejection of all complementarity, are forms of spiritual homosexuality.

3. The separation of the Catholic and Orthodox Churches is a great sin, but Divine Providence has permitted this separation so as to extract from it a superior good: to allow the Church of Christ to discover within herself all the human and divine richness of the Incarnation and the Redemption.

   "More generally, we can affirm that for human knowledge and human action a certain dialectic is present," writes John Paul II. "Did not the Holy Spirit, in His divine 'condescendence,' take this into

50

consideration? It is necessary for humanity to achieve unity through plurality, to learn to come together in the one Church, even while presenting a plurality of ways of thinking and acting, of cultures and civilizations. Wouldn't such a way of looking at things be, in a certain sense, more consonant with the wisdom of God, with His goodness and providence? Nevertheless, this cannot be a justification for the divisions that continue to deepen! The time must come for the love that unites us to be manifested!"[30]

Vladimir Soloviev[31] is the first to pose the question of unity in these terms. His philosophy, both theoretical and practical, is based on the concept of all-unity (*vseedinstvo*), which can be summarized as follows: maximum unity in maximum multiplicity. For him, the general has meaning only to the extent it accommodates the particular, and the particular only has meaning to the extent it accommodates the general. For Soloviev, unity can only be the unity of the totality. A unity which does not respect multiplicity, as well as a diversity which refuses to create within it a place for unity, is nothing but an abstraction and a lie.[32]

☆

The Church of the 19th century was not ready for such a message—and Soloviev knew it. He writes for the men and women of the 21st century, for those who survived the cataclysms of the 20th century, which he foresaw.

The Polish pope is the great intellectual and cultural heir of this Russian philosopher. In 2000, on the occasion of the centennial of Soloviev's death, he writes: "In remembering this Russian personality of extraordinary profundity, who clearly perceived the drama of the division of Christians, and of the urgent need for unity, I would invite the world to pray that the Christians of the East and the West return as quickly as possible to full communion."[33]

☆

The thought of Karol Wojtyla is profoundly Eastern. It is not linear, like that of his predecessors, but circular. With John Paul II, one always returns to the point of departure.

This "creative nostalgia" is the strength of the East. The East is an eagle; its trajectory is an ascending spiral. The West is a lion; its trajectory is that of an arrow. The eagle and the lion are two symbols of greatness perceived from different angles.

☆

During my university years, it is John Paul II who shapes my thinking.

Later, I would have the chance to be in his presence, to listen to him and speak to him in Rome, Helsinki and Tallinn.

John Paul II, like Escriva, is a giant. For me, he is also a father and a master.

# PARIS

I grew up in Paris and went to school there. I also discovered my vocation there. I owe Paris everything.

☆

I admire France.

In France, one learns to break the chains of conventional thought, to overcome stultified traditions, to flee the boring monotony of the *déjà vu.*

"Why does France continue to occupy the first place in Europe?" asks Dostoevsky. "Because she is always the country to take the first step, to make the first experiment, to have the first idea."[34]

I think of the ingenious idea of European integration, not in its current form—degraded, devoid of its original content, a travesty of its founders' intent—but as it was conceived by Jean Monnet and Robert Schuman: a profoundly moral idea entailing a noble vision of the human person.

☆

My friend Alex Coeurderoy incarnates the greatness of France.

We meet in the third year of law school. I am struck by his nobility of spirit and love for the great French tradition (which does not prevent him from poking good-natured fun at its occasional pomposity). He has a profound sense of duty and great personal dignity. His heart is free and filled with certainty. From the age of 15, he knew Blandine would be his wife. He makes bold decisions and never goes back on them. Coeurderoy goes through life at full tilt, jumping over all obstacles with the superhuman strength he derives from his Christian faith. Appropriately, Coeurderoy, or *coeur de roi,* means "heart of a king." He is my best friend from my university years.

☆

I love Paris—but with deep bitterness in my heart.

When I think of the French capital, I think of both Voltaire—that repulsive figure with his diabolical sneer who was the father of militant secularism, utterly intolerant and fanatical—and Rousseau—that sentimental, completely inconsistent father of naturalism (which denies the existence of evil in man and the necessity of self-improvement) and democratic totalitarianism (which does not recognize any truth higher than formal democracy).

Both men are entombed in the Panthéon, a secular mausoleum containing the remains of famous French citizens the state regards as its gods. An inscription above the main entrance reads: "To the great Men—the grateful Fatherland."

One reads the inscription and weeps because it is a lie—and in such wretched taste! The Panthéon, which had been a church dedicated to Geneviève, the patron saint of Paris who saved the city from Attila the Hun,[35] was rededicated after the French Revolution to "great Men," many of whom in reality were enemies of humanity.

☆

I have often pondered these words of Nikolai Berdyaev: "Paris is the city of the new Europe, and of new European humanity. … Paris is the city of the sublime harmony of the old and the new. … But Paris is also the city of a *petit-bourgeois* spirit, which is the fruit of an insatiable thirst for pleasure. … The free play of human energies, independent of any higher principle and sense of the sacred has resulted in the triumph of the *petit-bourgeois* spirit. … The *petit-bourgeois* spirit is a metaphysical category, not a social one. Socialism is penetrated by this spirit and is fundamentally atheist and irreligious. … After great sorrows and great upheavals, the heroic spirit of the French will awaken. The end of the *petit-bourgeois* spirit, of its irreligiousness and contempt for religion, is inevitable. Paris will be born again to new life. The salvation of France is one of Russia's great, universal tasks."[36]

☆

The message of Fatima pertains not just to Russia but to France as well.

In 1931, at Rianjo, Spain, Jesus Christ complained to Lucia that the consecration of Russia to the Immaculate Heart of Mary, requested in 1929, had not yet taken place: "They did not want to listen to my request. Like the King of France, they will repent for it."

In 1689, through the intermediation of Saint Margaret Mary, Christ asked King Louis XIV to consecrate France to his Sacred Heart. Blinded by his passions and drunk on pride, he died without having answered the divine request. Nor did his successors—Louis XV or Louis XVI—carry out the consecration.

In 1789, the French Revolution broke out, followed in 1792 by the persecution of the Church. In 1793, Louis XVI was decapitated in full public view.

France should be consecrated to the Heart of Jesus and Russia to the Heart of Mary. That is God's plan. France and

Russia are the objects of divine favor and their destinies are inseparable. As inseparable as the Sacred Heart of Jesus and the Immaculate Heart of Mary.

God, France, Russia—these formed the substance and framework of my deepest, most intimate thoughts. These are what have filled my heart for a long, long time.

# HELSINKI

I complete my legal studies in 1985 in Paris.

I spend my military service (which was obligatory at the time in France) teaching Russian language and literature at the Lycée Militaire de Saint-Cyr[37] near Paris. During my free time, I study for the entrance exam to the Centre de Formation Professionelle des Avocats, the French equivalent of the bar association.

☆

In 1985, I leave Paris for Strasbourg to begin my career as a lawyer. As I handle a number of criminal cases, I have to call on some of my clients in prison.

My first client shot his best friend in the head during a bout of heavy drinking. The victim's brains wound up on the ceiling. My other client is a Turk, who decapitated his father-in-law with a kitchen knife.

These cases are tragi-comic, but others are just tragic: A mother and father, tired of the incessant crying of their new-born baby, stash him in the refrigerator. He freezes to death.

☆

In Strasbourg, I make the acquaintance of the widow of Fyodor Fyodorovich Raskolnikov, who was one of the Old

57

Bolsheviks. He joined the Communist Party as a student in 1910 in Saint Petersburg—seven years before the Bolsheviks seized power. In 1920, he became the commander of the Soviet Union's Baltic fleet and, in 1936, the Soviet ambassador to Bulgaria. One day in 1938, while changing flights at an airport in Berlin on a trip from Sophia to Moscow, he read a newspaper story about his imminent dismissal as ambassador. That was news to him. He understood perfectly well that this meant he had fallen out of favor and that the press report was tantamount to a death sentence. This was the time of Stalin's purges of the Old Bolsheviks. So Roskolnikova and his wife got on the next airplane headed in the opposite direction—to Paris. A year later, he committed suicide in Nice—or was he killed by agents of the NKVD (the precursor of the KGB)?

His widow, Muza Vassilievna Raskolnikova, invites me to her house for dinner. We talk. I listen with interest but realize straight away that we have nothing in common.

Strasbourg is only a pit-stop in the trajectory of my life. In June 1989, I leave for Finland. I am 27 years old.

It is the Holy Spirit who is calling me to Nordic Europe.

Several days after my arrival in Helsinki, for the first time in history, a pope lands in Finland. He kisses the soil.

John Paul II did not come to Finland to visit Santa Claus, who in any case lives in the far north of the country near the Russian border. Addressing politicians and diplomats in Helsinki, Pope Wojtyla declares: "My coming to this Finlandia Hall is intended to manifest once again my strong support for the process which was set in motion in this very place on August 1, 1975 at the Conference on Security and Cooperation in Europe. *The Helsinki Final Act,* signed by the nations of Europe, together with Canada and the United

States, must be considered as one of the most significant of the instruments of international dialogue. ... At the Helsinki Conference, the negotiators upheld the principle that believers who feel discriminated against because of their faith, or who fear adverse reactions when they practice that faith, cannot share fully in the construction of the society in which they live. When basic human rights and freedoms are repressed, the social harmony of an entire nation is in some way disturbed. As a result, the work of peace is hindered."[38]

Everyone understands that the pope is referring to the Soviet Union.

Five months later, in November 1989, the Berlin Wall comes down.

☆

In 1990, as the USSR begins to disintegrate, I make a trip to Tbilisi, Soviet Georgia, for the first time since 1983, when I visited Elena and her son, Thamaz. In the interim, my great-aunt passed away, leaving Thamaz alone.

One evening, Thamaz and I decide to visit her grave. So we drive there, with Thamaz at the wheel of our Soviet-made Zhiguli. He loves his mother more than anyone else on earth. He has never left her since the traumatic day in 1938 when his father was arrested and shot by the Communist secret police.

The closer we get to the cemetery, the more emotional Thamaz becomes. The road is bad. It is a narrow, rain-slick-ened mountain road, and the sky is pitch black. Suddenly, Thamaz turns towards me: "Are you afraid?" Ashamed to say otherwise, I reply, "No!" He steps on the accelerator.

I hardly have time to invoke my guardian angel when the car goes off the road, sails out over an abyss and lands some seconds later in the heart of a mountain cemetery. The windshield shatters to bits. The Zhiguli winds up suspended between two headstones. I extract myself from the car gingerly so as not to upset the balance. Several yards away there is a deep ravine.

We go back down the mountain on foot, in silence, without

encountering a single vehicle. Thamaz finally says: "It's a shame we didn't accomplish what we set out to do and demolished some graves, which didn't belong to us."

An hour later, we hitch a ride back to Tbilisi. It is two o'clock in the morning.

This misadventure ended badly; it could have ended much worse. This man of sixty-five years of age had long ago—probably at the age of 10—lost all sense of orientation and of life as such.

Often I think of Thamaz and the millions of people wounded in one way or another by the ideological projects of the 20th century. I think of the emptiness, the devastation they produced in hearts, and of current global policies, which by focusing obsessively on economics only aggravate these wounds.

☆

In December 1989, shortly after having established myself in Helsinki, I receive a phone call from my cousin Nicolas. This 24-year-old Frenchman is working for Nokia in Salo, a city 100 kilometers from Helsinki. He is taken aback by the cold, the darkness, the solitude. … He dreamed of coming to Finland; now he finds himself in the desert of reality. He goes through a deep spiritual crisis, which with God's help he soon overcomes. His friendship means a lot to me during my first year in Finland.

☆

On May 11, 1990, I take the ferry boat from Helsinki to St. Petersburg (then still called Leningrad.) On May 12, the eve of the feast of Our Lady of Fatima, I set foot for the first time in the capital of the former Russian Empire.

I go to the apartment houses occupied in the 1910s by my grandfather Pavel, on Kirochnaya Street, and by my grandmother Nina, on Vassilevskiy Island. The original buildings still stand. Moved, I try to imagine both places as they must have been 70 years ago.

☆

The first people I meet are Sasha and Lyuba Shipkov and their four children. I have lunch with them at their place in Labutina Street. Sasha is a journalist. In 1979, his mother— Tatiana Shipkova, philologist and professor of romance languages—was sentenced to three years in prison for speaking to her students about Jesus Christ. The charge was hooliganism.

I had gotten Sasha's address from Irina Ilovaiskaya-Alberti, the director of the Paris-based, Russian and French-language newspaper Russkaya Mysl' (La Pensée Russe). She is a remarkable woman. She defends the oppressed, especially those persecuted for their religious views. She speaks ten languages fluently and was Aleksandr Solzhenitsyn's secretary for three years during his exile in Vermont.[39]

When I think of Irina, I also think of her cat. Every time I go to her office in Paris, I come down with an allergy attack so violent I am laid up for several days.

☆

In St. Petersburg, I make the acquaintance of my cousins, the Ordzhonikidzes—distant relatives of the aforementioned Sergo Ordzhonikidze, an early Bolshevik and one of Stalin's henchmen. Lali, a Georgian cousin of mine in Tbilisi, gave me their coordinates. I call them from a telephone booth in the city center:

- Misha Ordzhonikidze?
- *Yes!*
- This is Alex, your cousin from Finland.
- *Our cousin from Finland?*
- Lali from Tbilisi gave me your phone number.
- *Come for lunch. We'll be expecting you.*

I climb the staircase of the beautiful but dilapidated apartment house, built in Tsarist times, on Suvorovskiy Prospekt across from the former General Staff Military Academy. My cousins live on the top floor. The doorbell bears not one but four names: Ivanov (one ring), Petrov (two rings), Andreev (three rings) and Ordzhonikidze (four rings).

It is a Soviet communal apartment with four families living in a single flat.

I ring four times. Misha Ordzhonikidze opens the door and introduces me to his wife Valya and their son, Soso. We enter a room that serves as their living and dining room. On the table, there are several bottles of wine and vodka. My cousins are ready to make merry. For them, I am like a son they haven't seen for years who has returned from afar. And yet, half an hour ago, they had no idea I even existed.

We begin to drink and tell stories around the dining room table, while another family prepares dinner in the adjacent common kitchen.

Misha is Georgian. After the war, he moved to Leningrad where he met Valya, a Russian. Both taught Marxist sociology at the university for many years. They were members of the Communist Party until leaving it a year ago. Misha is agnostic. Valya was baptized recently. Misha says that until not too long ago, the secret police would give him lists of students to be expelled from the university for their religious views. Valya gets angry: "You don't have to tell Alex things like *that!*"

☆

In his address in Finland, Pope John Paul II talks about more than just the USSR. He also talks about Europe and its prevalent "culture of death." It is already politically *incorrect* to reject abortion and euthanasia, and the media are just beginning to promote the cloning of human embryos and the adoption of children by homosexual couples.

In April 1991, I organize an international conference in Helsinki in defense of the "culture of life." I invite Jérôme Lejeune, the French geneticist who discovered the genetic origins of Down Syndrome in 1958. He is a friend. We met several years before at the National Congress for the Family in Strasbourg.

Just before the start of our conference, I receive an unexpected phone call from a woman of considerable influence in Finland. She says she knows Lejeune and makes no bones about the fact that she detests him. She insults me. She accuses me of organizing an "ideological" conference without her authorization. She says I seek to undermine the foundations of Finnish society. She threatens me.

I smash the receiver onto its cradle, shouting in disgust: "Soviet Finland!"

Jérôme Lejeune speaks and sheds light on one of the most contentious topics of our time:

> "Modern genetics shows that from the moment the ovary is fertilized by the sperm, all the genetic information which defines the new individual is inscribed, in its entirety, in the first cell. No other genetic fact enters the egg after the initial fertilization. Thus, science affirms that a human being would not be a human being if he had not originally been conceived as a human being. If a law is so unfounded as to declare that a human embryo is not a human being, and that Her Majesty, the Queen of England, was only a chimpanzee during the first fourteen days of her life, it is not a law but a manipulation of opinion. No one is obliged to accept science. You can say: 'Fine, we prefer to be ignorant, we absolutely reject all scientific discoveries.' It's a point of view. I would say it's a 'politically correct' point of view, but it's an obscurantist point of view, and science abhors obscurantism."[40]

In the first row of the audience, a woman is smiling. It is not the woman who threatened me on the telephone several days before. That one did not attend because she did not dare: Flying in the face of science before a live audience is not a winning proposition. The smiling lady in the audience is Päivi Räsänen. She is a doctor and a writer. In a few months, she will go into politics and eventually become president of the Christian Democratic Party and Minister of the Interior. Räsänen is a woman who loves life, God and country. She is a courageous woman who loves the sinner but will have no truck with sin.

☆

I work in a law office in Helsinki. I learn Finnish.

Lenin made his final preparations for the Bolshevik seizure of power in Helsinki. Every time I go to church, I pass by an image of this devil on a commemorative plaque on the apartment house in Vuorimiehenkatu in which he lived for a time.

Lenin … on the way to church.

On the exterior wall of the Catholic cathedral, there is an enormous crucifix. It faces the Embassy of the Soviet Union on the other side of the street.

☆

On November 6, 1991, Boris Yeltsin, President of the Russian Soviet Federative Socialist Republic forbids the activities of the Communist Party within the Russian Federation. On December 25, 1991, Mikhail Gorbachev steps down as President of the Soviet Union. The next day, the Soviet Union is officially dissolved.

☆

I travel to St. Petersburg frequently by boat, train or bus, according to my convenience. I need to inhale the air of Russia and come face to face with Russian realities. Here is one such instance, which I recounted in the preface to my first book on leadership:

> "It occurred on a bus journey from St. Petersburg to Helsinki on a bitterly cold winter's morning in 1992, not long after the fall of communism. It was a time of plunging industrial production, skyrocketing inflation

64

and rampant unemployment throughout the former Soviet Union. Elderly Russians found themselves in especially dire straits as inflation wiped out their already inadequate pensions. Many were reduced to collecting discarded bottles from waste bins for the deposit money. It was the only way to survive.

As the Finland-bound bus sped through what remained of Russia, I was struck by the contrast between the pristine winter landscape hurtling past my window and the less than edifying moral atmosphere on board. The passenger is front of me was sloshed. He appeared to be comatose.

The passenger to my right regaled me with sordid tales of a lost weekend of carousing. He wanted to offer me a cigarette, but thrust his hand in the wrong pocket and came up with a pack of condoms.

Our bus put in for a half-hour rest stop in front of the railway station at Vyborg, the last Russian city before the Finnish frontier. With the sun shining brightly on newly fallen snow, I bundled up and set out to explore the district around the station.

Presently, I came upon an old lady rummaging through a large pile of refuse to find something she could use, sell or cash-in for the deposit money. I reached into my pocket and came up with my few remaining rubles: 'Babushka[41], please take these.' She looked me straight in the eye and smiled radiantly. Anxious not to miss the bus, I made my way quickly back to the station.

Just I as I was stepping aboard, I heard a voice behind me. I wheeled around. It was the old lady trundling towards me as fast as she could, with a beaming smile on her face and a large bouquet of flowers in her out-stretched hand. I accepted it. She left without saying a word.

We crossed the border leaving my beloved Russia

behind. I laid back and closed my eyes and reflected on what this woman had done: Although indigent, she bought the flowers with the money I had given her, and with no certainty that she would find me. She could have used the money to have a nice dinner; instead, she bought me a gift, and because this was not from her surplus, made a gift of herself to me. I was overcome with joy, with a deep love for life, with a desire to convert, to purify my heart, to be better."[42]

☆

Here is another Russian story, although perhaps less edifying:

The scene unfolds in the night train between the Estonian capital of Tallinn and Moscow. I share a compartment with a Russian from Estonia who tells me that not so long ago he served a five-year prison sentence for theft, but that, *in principle,* he had since changed his ways.

I see he is taking pills and ask him if he is sick. "No," he says, "these are to prevent me from stealing again, to avoid the temptation."

I can hardly believe my ears. This man is taking pills so as not to rip-off his traveling companions.

Well, the medication did not work. During the night he stole all of my money with amazing *savoir-faire* and *legerdemain.*

I confront him. He does not admit to his crime. I cannot believe this is happening.

He generously gives me 50 rubles for subway fare when we get to Moscow!

I go straight to the Ugandan Embassy on Momonovsky Street, where Ambassador Christopher Onyanga Appar, an old friend, puts me up for the night. Together we pray the Holy Rosary for Russia.

☆

Roughly a dozen of us live at the Opus Dei center in Helsinki. We are from Stockholm, Paris, Bilbao, Cologne, Valencia, Granada and Buenos Aires. Half of us are students. I am 30 years old and one of the oldest residents. Almost everyone living there plays a musical instrument and can sing: Finnish pop music, Spanish flamenco, Russian folk songs, Sinatra, Leonard Cohen—you name it.

We speak Finnish among ourselves. I find the sense of humor of these young people astonishing—a humor that transcends and transfigures the reality all around. This humor unifies us, welds us together. Such a sense of humor I have never encountered anywhere else. It is a gift of God, a manifestation of His grace to help us overcome the austerity and, indeed, the severity of the Finnish temperament.

☆

The Finns are an astonishing people.

Whether rich or poor, all a Finn needs to be happy is a small house with a sauna on one of Finland's 187,888 lakes. He requires nothing more.

Finns do not know how to lie, although they sometimes have trouble telling all of the truth. Because they are timid, they have trouble being sincere and opening their hearts. They often fear what others will say. They fear not thinking the way everyone else does, not feeling and acting just as others do.

☆

Everyone here loves cold weather and the snow, but not everyone loves the long winter nights.[43] I find them enchanting. I love walking through the still, snowy city at dusk, my path illuminated by the warm glow of Christmas lights.

☆

Nature hereabouts is pure and beautiful. The contrasts are surprising, the variations in landscape subtle.

In the summer, I spend hours working, reading and meditating at isolated spots along the Gulf of Finland. And swimming—I swim until I no longer can.

☆

I receive a letter from Tobias, whom I had prepared for the sacrament of Confirmation when he was 13 years old. That was in Strasbourg. Now 28 years old, he is a graduate of the Institut d'Études Politiques in Paris. He is coming to visit me in February.

I want him to experience the delights of the Nordic winter. So, along with some friends, we rent a small house for the weekend on an island in the Gulf of Finland. The air is frigid, and the sea is frozen, with the exception of a channel cut by a ferryboat that runs every hour between the island and the mainland.

One evening, we partake of the traditional Finnish sauna. After half an hour of intense heat, Tobias and I decide to walk across the ice and jump into the channel to cool down—a typical practice. But we did not foresee the problem of getting out of the water and back onto the ice. There is no ladder and the edge of the ice is slippery. After several unsuccessful attempts to exit the frigid waters, we are seized with the realization that, absent a miracle, we will be dead within minutes.

At least we have the consolation of knowing that a deep night, a half moon and a million stars will accompany us during our last moments of earthly existence. Tobias and I are paying a steep price for our imprudence. But then I notice that the freezing wind beating on my wet skin has caused my arms to stick to the ice. This gives me leverage to haul my legs up onto the ice. Then I reach down and pull Tobias out of the water. We live to tell the tale.

☆

With the exception of tragicomic adventures of this kind, life is fairly humdrum.

The years pass and nothing happens.

Or so it seems outwardly. In reality, these are years of great spiritual intensity.

I often meditate on the words of Escriva: "What does it matter that you have to curtail your activity for the moment, if later, like a spring which has been compressed, you'll advance much farther than you ever dreamed?"[44]

Saint Josemaria wrote these words in 1937 as civil war engulfed Spain. He and several of his spiritual sons took refuge in the small Honduran Embassy in Madrid. For him and his sons, this period of forced inactivity was a time of unimaginable spiritual growth.

I live in Finland for 18 years and 24 days.

# TALLINN-VILNIUS

In the 1990s, I travel to Tallinn, the capital of Estonia, once a month. In winter, the Gulf of Finland is often frozen. It is a long trip as the bow of the ice-breaker slowly cuts through the narrow channel.

But this Arctic desert warms up when the sun shines, causing smiles to break out on the severe Finno-Ugric faces of the passengers. The light, reflecting off the icy surface of the sea, is so strong you think it is summer.

I teach European law at Tallinn Law School. I am glad that my students have been freed from communism, but it pains me to see them embrace consumerism and hedonism.

A new world is being born. Communism is dead, but the liberal materialism that gave rise to it lives on. No one reflects on the causes of communism. People here live from day to day and adapt to the new rules of the game with astonishing ease.

In my law course, I try to give orientation to my students and instill ideals. Some listen to me with interest; others look

at me with eyes full of pity—as though I were the hippopot-
amus in a zoo.

☆

I offer a course in Christian social philosophy. It is free of
charge so that anyone can attend. It is in Russian because
everyone understands Russian. The lecture hall is full.

Those who lived under communism know that the impact
of the "One, True Doctrine of Marxism-Leninism" on society
was vast and, by and large, deleterious. There is a big differ-
ence between seeing man as a child of God and seeing him
as closely related to an orangutan.

☆

I make the acquaintance of Lembit Peterson, who is a
theater professor and the director of an internationally
renowned theater. Lembit lived for 40 years under the
horror of communism. Now he lives under the horror of
liberalism. He was baptized in the Catholic Church during
Soviet times, when this was a highly provocative act. He has
never been afraid to take risks.

Lembit wants to save his people from moral anarchy. He
wants to give meaning to life. He puts on original plays that
make the spectator think. He speaks Russian and French
fluently. He knows both cultures well. He loves Chekhov
and Claudel. We spend lots of time together in Old Tallinn,
one of the most picturesque cities in the world. We discuss
our experience of communism and liberalism. Lembit had
three children during Soviet times and three more children
during the liberal period. He trusts in God. Numerous are
his students who were baptized into the Church. He is my
best friend in Estonia.

☆

In April 1993, Bishop (now, Blessed) Alvaro del Portillo is
in Helsinki. He decides to make a quick excursion to Tallinn.

Del Portillo became the head of Opus Dei upon the death

of its founder in 1975. He was consecrated a bishop by Pope John Paul II in 1991. It was he who gave me the green light to move to Finland in 1989. Now he asks me to accompany him to Tallinn.

The trip takes several hours. We are a group of just a few people. In Tallinn, we pray in the Catholic Cathedral of Saints Peter and Paul, in the Lutheran Church of the Holy Spirit and in the Orthodox Cathedral of Saint Alexander Nevsky, overlooking the city.

We get together with some Estonian friends in the library of the secondary school where Lembit works in the heart of the old city. It is a family reunion. We are seated around a low table.

Don Alvaro suffered the atrocities of communism in his flesh. When the Spanish Civil War broke out, he was 22 years old. He was imprisoned for the crime of being a Christian, subjected to physical and psychological torture, including being forced to eat human excrement. But Don Alvaro never spoke of such things; he spoke only of pardon and mercy.

By temperament, Alvaro del Portillo is the opposite of Josemaria Escriva, but in his character and virtues, he is his mirror image. Both men are exemplars of magnanimity— the concentration of heart, mind and will on the achievement of great goals.

☆

Don Alvaro's mission in life is to help Escriva realize the task God entrusted to him—the founding of Opus Dei. He does so with immense wisdom and generosity. Since the Founder's departure for heaven in 1975, Don Alvaro's mission, for the rest of his life, is to build the Work of God in exemplary faithfulness to the Founder's spirit. He is Saint Josemaria's most faithful son.

Our meeting in Tallinn is destined to be our last on this earth. He dies in Rome on March 23, 1994, several hours after having celebrated Holy Mass at the Cenacle in Jerusalem, the site of Christ's Last Supper. When Pope John Paul II hears the news of Don Alvaro's death, he goes to pray before his earthly remains in the oratory of Opus Dei's main house in Rome. Instead of reciting the traditional prayer for the dead (a prayer of supplication for the salvation of the soul of the deceased), he prays the Salve Regina in honor of the Mother of God and three Glorias in honor of the Holy Trinity. John Paul II, who knew Don Alvaro well, knew he was a saint, and saints do not need prayers of supplication for the salvation of their souls.[45]

One day, when I was 22 years old, Don Alvaro said to me with his typical warmth and simplicity: "Alexandre, I must rely on your strength." These words have always helped me remain faithful to the path I was on. But since he went to heaven, it is I who must rely on his strength, on the power of intercession of this spiritual giant of immense heart, who was for me a father and confidant.

In Estonia, I make the acquaintance of Maido Rahula, a mathematics professor at the University of Tartu—one of Europe's oldest centers of higher education. At the end of the Second World War, Maido, who is Estonian, was deported to Siberia with his family. He was 10 years old at the time. Later, he married Larissa, a Russian and also a mathematician, in the Siberian city of Krasnoyarsk. Although both were members of the Communist Party, they discovered Christianity under the influence of the theosophist thinker and artist Nikolai Rerikh,[46] who achieved a certain posthumous vogue in the USSR in the early 1990s. Maido became Lutheran and Larissa became Orthodox. Both are great admirers of Saint Josemaria Escriva.

Maido, who is a world-renowned specialist in catastrophe theory, interprets Escriva's message through the prism of this theory. I do not understand a word he is talking about.

Larissa is dying of cancer. She is at peace: She confessed her sins several months before at the Marian shrine of

Torrecuidad in the Spanish Pyrenees. It was the first and last confession of her life.

She invites her friends to her house to talk about God. They find her prostrate on a chaise longue.

One of them is another Larissa—Larissa Volpert—who is Jewish. Originally from Leningrad, she won the Soviet chess championship for women three times. She is now a professor of French literature at the University of Tartu.

Larissa Volpert listens to Larissa Rahula, prone on her chaise longue, as she speaks of Escriva.

A dozen of us are arranged around Larissa Rahula. All are seeking God, each in his or her own manner.

Several days after Western Christmas, we bury Larissa in the Orthodox cemetery of Tartu. It is 25 degrees below zero centigrade (minus 16 degrees Fahrenheit). The sun is shining.

Several months later, the first Opus Dei center opens in Tallinn.

☆

I travel regularly to Vilnius, the capital of Lithuania.

Proponents of the culture of death have drafted a law authorizing artificial insemination. It has the backing of a number of big capitalists who, until recently, were big Communists. The aim is to make big money selling aborted Lithuanian babies to overseas buyers at prices well below those of the competition.

Donatas, a doctor in Vilnius who finds liberalism as repugnant as communism, is organizing a rally in defense of life in Vilnius. He asks me to deliver a speech criticizing the draft law from a legal point of view.

He says I should address the crowd in English, but since Lithuania was a part of the Soviet Union until just 10 years before, I suggest it might be better if I spoke Russian. At the rally, I ask the audience which language they would prefer. With a loud roar, the public expressed its preference for Russian. So we employ the language of Pushkin, which had been used in Lithuania for 50 years to impose a diabolical ideology, to defend human dignity in the liberal era.

At the outset, the authors of the draft version of the law on artificial insemination mention the "interests of children."

I tell the crowd: "The 'interests of children' is a demagogic formula that reminds me of the preamble to the Soviet Constitution and its wholly illusory claim to promote a 'genuine democracy for the working masses.'"

The culture of death "loves" children just as communism "loved" workers. This draft is a tissue of lies and manipulation.

I speak of Jérôme Lejeune and his scientific and moral witness, which is known around the world.

The proposed law of 2003 went down to defeat. Donatas won the battle.

☆

Four years later, I receive a phone call from Vilnius. It is Donatas: "Alex, the culture of death is counterattacking. Brussels wants to impose same-sex marriage. I am organizing a conference in the parliament in defense of the family. We are expecting you."

I fly to Vilnius.

I speak in English: "The Bolsheviks, in applying Marxist theories, tried for 70 years to liquidate the natural institution of the family. Alexandra Kollontaï[47] and Anatoliy Lunacharskiy[48] are two names, which sadly have gone down in history. The family policy of the European parliament is nothing but the continuation of their policies."

Again, Donatas prevails. The Lithuanian parliament soon confirms what we all know: The family is the matrimonial union of a man and a woman together with their children.

☆

When I am in Vilnius, I always visit a chapel on the upper floor of the last remaining of the city's old defensive gates called the Gate of Dawn. It contains an icon of the Virgin

Mary, Mother of Mercy, which dates to the 16th century, and seems to dominate the city: She can be seen clearly through the chapel's large Palladian window from a great distance. Painted in the Byzantine manner, the image is venerated by Catholics and Orthodox alike.

I ask the Mother of God always the same thing: that she open the doors of Russia—the Gate of Dawn—to the Work of God.

# MISSION

In the mid-1990s, the University of Helsinki asks me to give a course in French on European Law. Half of the lectures deal with the history of European integration in order to help students come to grips with the thought of the European Union's founding fathers: Robert Schuman, Jean Monnet, Konrad Adenauer and Alcide de Gasperi.

My students love it. They open themselves up, they speak, they react spontaneously. Many thank me privately for teaching things no one else at the university would talk about.

I give my students *information*, but I am more concerned with their formation. I want them to expand their hearts. I speak of the moral virtues of Europe's founding fathers. I want my students to contemplate these virtues, discover their intrinsic beauty and try to practice them.

Professional competence is not only the result of theoretical or practical knowledge, it also stems from the assiduous formation of character and from moral habits firmly rooted in the heart, mind and will. The modern university puts the accent more and more on *information*, and less and less on *education* in the broad sense of the term. It produces managers rather than leaders, knowledge rather than wisdom, techniques rather than courage. It concerns itself more and more with things, and less and less with persons. The crisis of the modern world is not a crisis of information, it is a crisis of formation, a crisis of authentic education.

I am passionate about leadership: Not leadership as a technique based on styles and methods, but the natural leadership that is based on character. The leadership that interests me is fundamental leadership, the leadership of always, leadership such as it was perceived in antiquity.

I immerse myself in Aristotelian, Confucian and Judeo-Christian anthropology. I analyze the lives and actions of the great figures of politics, business, science, religion, literature and sports.

I elaborate a system of leadership in which magnanimity (greatness) and humility (service) are the virtues specific to leadership, while courage, prudence, self-control and justice constitute its foundation. I conceive of leadership as the science that allows us to achieve greatness by bringing out the greatness in others.

I seek out men and women who correspond to this model. I meet Aleksandr Solzhenitsyn at his home in Moscow, Lech Walesa at his office in Gdansk, François Michelin at his company's headquarters in Clermont-Ferrand, and Jérôme Lejeune, the great geneticist and a good friend, at his apartment in Paris.

☆

It is October 6, 2002. I am in Saint Peter's Square in Rome. Pope John Paul II is presiding over the canonization of Josemaria Escriva, with 400,000 pilgrims in attendance from all over the world.

With me are Sergei from St. Petersburg and Alik from Moscow.

Sergei is a 30-year-old economist. Several years ago, he knew next to nothing about Christianity. I gave him private instruction. He developed a strong devotion to Saint Josemaria.

Alik Zorin is an accomplished poet and a member of the Writers' Union since 1979. A Christian believer, his spiritual father was the eminent Orthodox priest Aleksandr Men, who was assassinated in 1990 by a man wielding an ax as Father Aleksandr was on his way to celebrate the liturgy. Father Aleksandr introduced Zorin to the spirituality of Escriva during the late Brezhnev years, when religious news and information were rigorously suppressed.

Zorin remembers a clandestine meeting with parishioners at Father Aleksandr's home in the spring of 1980: "Father Aleksandr mentioned the name of Josemaria Escriva, which none of those present recognized. We often recorded these meetings on tape, including, happily, this one. Here is what he said: 'For the past several decades, there has existed in the West an organization called Opus Dei, the Work of God. Its founder is the Spanish priest Josemaría Escriva. The organization is extensive and found everywhere. He wrote a small book called *The Way,* which is a collection of aphorisms. Escriva says that to be a Christian does not mean to live like a Philistine, a *petit-bourgeois* or a heathen and on Sundays go somewhere at a set time for spiritual uplift. A Christian is a Christian at all times, every day, in the most ordinary circumstances, dealing with the most ordinary things.'"

By sheer coincidence, a copy of *The Way,* which was circulating underground in samizdat,[49] falls into Zorin's hands later that year. Typewritten on cigarette paper, it has been passed from hand to hand. It is now in a fragile condition and hardly legible.

Zorin, in turn, introduces Escriva to a national audience in an article for the Muscovite daily newspaper Segodnya (August 27, 1994.)

☆

John Paul II delivers the sermon at the canonization Mass of Josemaria Escriva: "Raise the world towards God and transform it from inside: This is the ideal which the saint-founder sets before you, beloved brothers and sisters."

The next day, also in Saint Peter's Square, at the Mass of Thanksgiving for the canonization of Saint Josemaria, the pope receives Patriarch Teoctist, the highest authority in the Romanian Orthodox Church. The throng is surprised by the appearance of such a high-ranking Orthodox prelate and explodes with joy when it sees him. Sergei and Alik, who are Orthodox, are deeply moved.

John Paul II says to Teoctist: "I wanted your visit to begin in the context of this general audience, in the presence of so many faithful, who have come from all over the world. The people participating in this meeting are members of Opus Dei. They have come to give thanks for the canonization of their founder, Escriva de Balaguer. I believe they are happy. May these days nourish our dialogue and fortify our hope. May they make us more conscious of that which unites us, of the common roots of our faith, of our liturgical patrimony, of the saints and martyrs we have in common. May the Lord make us feel once again how beautiful and sweet it is to invoke Him together."

☆

I turn 40 years old. I begin teaching my system of leadership in Finland, the Baltic States, Poland, Russia, the United States and Kenya. I teach executives, college students, and directors of schools. I teach in English and Russian, and sometimes in French and Spanish.

My first seminar, offered on a commercial basis, takes place in Tallinn in August 2004. The participants are directors of secondary schools. Lembit Peterson, my Estonian friend, plays a key role in organizing the seminar.

I am a writer, but above all I am a teacher: I communicate my message with my body, not just with my pen.

☆

My first book, *Virtuous Leadership,* is published in 2007 in New York. Between 2007 and 2012, it is translated into 14 languages.

The appearance of the Chinese edition, published by the Social Sciences Academic Press, the publishing wing of the Chinese Academy of Social Sciences, fills me with joy: My system of leadership is not European but universal in character. It is certainly inspired by Christianity, but Christianity is the most natural and universal of all religions because it is the only religion that is true *in its totality.* Christian anthropology is comprehensible by all peoples; it assimilates, completes and unifies all of the truths about man that have been discovered since time immemorial.

I have only one professional ambition: to spread through the entire world a concept of leadership that corresponds to the most authentic demands of human nature and the noblest aspirations of the human heart. I have only one desire—to inflame hearts, to inspire men and women to embrace the ideals of greatness and service, to contribute to the creation of a new generation of leaders called to transform life, culture and business, and thus to lay the foundations for a new civilization.

I make new friends on four continents who share my sense of urgency about the world's need for virtuous leaders. Together, we open Virtuous Leadership Centers in Moscow, Washington, Shanghai and Nairobi.

# MOSCOW

Beginning in 1992, I direct the team that translates the works of Saint Josemaria Escriva into Russian. By 2002, the work of translation has been completed, and a dozen books have been published in Moscow. The quality of the translations is exceptional. It is the work of Natalia Trauberg, Nadezhda Muravyova and Alik Zorin—all gifted translators and talented writers in their own right.

*The Way* is the first book of the founder of Opus Dei. It is his major work. First published in 1934, five million copies have been printed since then. *"The Way,"* says Alik Zorin, "is the work of a poet. The dynamism, the rhythm, the energy that emerge from each page is the energy proper to poetry. In *The Way,* one finds the poetics of the Book of Wisdom and the Book of Proverbs. Escriva's teachings are dense, aphoristic, close to didactic poetry. Translated into Russian, they retain the nuances of poetic discourse, which enriches the meaning and the content—a content very close and intimate to the Russian soul."[50]

Nevertheless, the first book of Josemaria Escriva to be published in Russia was not *The Way* but *Way of the Cross.* That is what Divine Providence wanted, because the Passion of Christ is a way of suffering and also a way of hope and victory. Russia, having experienced its Golgotha, is approaching the hour of its resurrection and triumph.

In his book *Furrow,* written in the 1940s, Escriva had a presentiment of this victory: He speaks of Russia as "this nation, so arid today, but which, with time, will produce immense fields of wheat."[51]

Towards the end of the 1990s, a group of friends and I launch a social action program in the Moscow and St. Petersburg areas. Some thirty students from several European countries come together every year to help refurbish the dilapidated dwellings of poor families and rebuild churches destroyed under communism.

The program is hard work, but not only: On weekends, the European students call on inmates at local prisons. Once, we visit the prison in Tikhvin, 200 kilometers east of St. Petersburg. The prison warden invites our Irish students to play a soccer match with the young Russian prisoners. These forgotten ones of Russia are moved by the disinterested and unexpected friendliness of perfect strangers.

☆

On April 18, 2006, Bishop Javier Echevarria, who is the second successor to Saint Josemaria Escriva as the head of Opus Dei, sets foot on Russian soil for the first time.

His visit begins on the Tuesday after Western Easter Sunday and ends the following Sunday, which happens to be Orthodox Easter and which is also the Catholic feast of Divine Mercy. He visits Moscow and St. Petersburg. He prays intensely in Catholic and Orthodox churches. A small group accompanies him.

He tells my friend Mikhail Fateev, a journalist from St. Petersburg: "After the resurrection of the Church in your country, responsibility for the resurrection of the Church in Europe and the whole world will rest with the Church in Russia."

☆

On June 25, 2007, I board the train at Helsinki Central Station for Moscow as I have done so often in the past. But this time, something is different—I have no return ticket.

That is because Don Javier Echevarria asked me to be part of the small team of members of Opus Dei to move to Russia. There are five of us—from Finland, Italy, Lithuania, Mexico and Spain.

By the time the train reaches Moscow, it is June 26. On that day I take up residency in the capital of Russia—the dream of a lifetime has come true, a prayer has been answered, a chapter in my life ends and a new one begins.

☆

Opus Dei is in Russia to learn and teach, to receive from the Russian people a new inspiration and new life, and to give the Russian people Saint Josemaria—his fatherhood and his spirit, which is rooted in the great tradition of the Church from the earliest days of Christianity.

☆

Russia is a country of martyrs. I know they intercede for us; I feel their presence all around me. The devil is determined to wipe out their influence, to render pointless the spilling of their blood for the sake of the Church.

☆

An Italian friend invites me to a restaurant in the center of Moscow. As we are speaking, a knife falls in a straight line from the mezzanine above, grazes my nose and breaks my plate in two. The waitress gives no explanation for this nearly fatal mishap, but in compensation she offers me a 20-percent discount.

☆

Between 2009 and 2011, I write a second book titled, *Created for Greatness: The Power of Magnanimity.*

*Created for Greatness* goes deeper into some of the ideas discussed in *Virtuous Leadership.* The two works are indivisible. *Created for Greatness* puts the accent on magnanimity (greatness) and humility (service), which are the virtues specific to leaders. In this book, I affirm that leadership is a life ideal that recognizes, assimilates and disseminates the truth about man. In addition, I give specific advice on how to develop these virtues.

With this second book, I complete the building of my system.

☆

I teach at universities and corporations in Moscow and St. Petersburg, and also in Kiev and Alma-Ata—the capitals of Ukraine and Kazakhstan, respectively—and I do not neglect Russia's other regions. I go to Novorossiysk on the Black Sea, Krasnodar in the steppes of Kuban, Nalchik in the North Caucasus, Kazan in Tatarstan, Ufa in Bashkiria, Novosibirsk in Western Siberia, Kaliningrad on the Baltic Sea, and elsewhere.

☆

"Now I understand the Russia that we lost in 1917," says a participant—the head of a major Moscow bank—at one of our virtuous leadership seminars. I am delighted to hear this, although I am well aware of the shortcomings of Tsarist Russia, which gave rise to the Bolshevik catastrophe.

My approach to leadership is profoundly Russian. My American, European, Chinese and African participants are surprised since the literature on this subject is mainly American. And yet here is a work of a pervasive Russian spirit, in which Russian sources abound. This is unexpected and indeed entirely new.

Leadership is not a technique but a way of being. Before asking "what should we do?", we need to ask "who are we and who should we *be*?" This is a profoundly moral question, one posed by all of 19th-century Russian literature. It is a question of critical importance to virtuous leadership.

Communism, like all ideologies, produced a human catastrophe: It strengthened the will (because it was focused on a goal) but destroyed the mind (by denying the natural order of things) and shriveled the heart (because it lived on false hopes.)

After 70 years of communism, peoples' hearts and minds are in need of restoration. The market economy expands the mind because it is concerned with meeting the *real* material needs of people. But it makes people more intelligent only in matters related to the market. We must complement this "material intelligence" with a "spiritual intelligence" so as to satisfy the most profound requirements of the human soul.

Unfortunately, when practical materialism replaces theoretical materialism (as, for example, when consumerism replaced Marxism-Leninism in the 1990s in Russia), it paralyzes the will. It inflames the vilest passions and makes it harder to practice the virtues of courage and self-control. It also makes the heart its slave: Consumption becomes the meaning and end of existence.

Twenty years have passed since the collapse of the Soviet Union, and the Russian heart, exhausted by ideology and enslaved by matter, nevertheless lives. It is reclaiming its lost rights.

Virtuous leadership is a response to this desperate cry of the soul.

☆

Virtue is a new concept for many people. For some, it has a clear fascination; for others—often skeptics and cynics with a dark vision of the human person—it is of little interest. But they are in the minority.

I come across men and women who seem to embrace virtue whole-heartedly but who in fact understand nothing—like the head of training for a Russian company, a woman and a participant in one of my seminars, who proposed that we sleep together.

It is the young, the students, who most easily grasp my message.

☆

Paris, March 2010. My brother Stéphane is laid to rest. He died in a deep-sea diving accident. He was 49. Thank you, God, for having given me a brother—a brother like Stéphane!

At the funeral, I meet Jacques, whom I have not seen in a quarter century. He is one of a number of old friends now living in homosexual relationships. Jacques has been living with his male partner for 10 years. They recently acquired a child through a surrogate mother in New York. Jacques sermonizes: "Alex, there are different ways to search for God. I think that you and I are closer spiritually than you think!"

When our conscience does not leave us in peace, when it troubles and even tortures us, we are tempted to escape our guilt by turning sin into something meritorious, converting vice into virtue and evil into good—all the while invoking God as if He would approve! Jacques! Jacques! Wake up, my friend. All is not lost. There is hope for you yet.

The West is sinking into the quicksand of a crass and viscous ideological obscurantism. What, meanwhile, will become of Russia? Will she be able to resist? And if she resists, will she be in any condition to save the West?

☆

I direct a leadership session for a Protestant group in St. Petersburg. One of the participants—Tamara, an artist—offers me some of her paintings as a gift. They are excellent. I ask her to paint a picture of my grandmother Nina's house on Saint Petersburg's Vassilevskiy Island. I give her the address.

She writes to me: "How marvelous to have had a house, a place of one's own, a home, and to remember it with affection! Noble emotions are always a gift of God. I have lived nearly all of my life in a communal apartment. For a long time, I refused to go near the street I used to live in. Recently, I passed by the house where your grandmother lived. Such a warm feeling came over me! No, it was not my house, or the house of a close relative of mine. But now I know what it means to have a home."

Nina indeed knew the warmth of a home. As she notes in her memoirs—movingly but also ironically: "Mother woke up very late. She had breakfast in bed, and had us come to her to kiss us. She spent lots of time at her vanity and did not leave her bedroom until around noon. It must be admitted that my mother did not know how to do anything—she neither sewed, nor cleaned the house, nor took care of the children. She was spared all this by her family who adored her."[52]

☆

In April 2004, I met Aleksandr Solzhenitsyn at his house in Troitse-Lykovo. He said to me: "You are the grandson of the first wave of emigrants, a representative of the third generation of Russians who lived abroad. To speak Russian the way you do, you must really love Russia."

This love of Russia was infused into my heart by the Holy Spirit when I was 15 years old.

☆

It is August 2, 2012. This morning, I am going to the immigration service. The Federal Security Service (FSB)—the successor organization to the Soviet KGB—has denied me a residency permit on the basis of Article 7.1 of the law governing the stay of foreigners in Russia, which the FSB interprets to mean that *my activities constitute a threat to the security of the Russian Federation.*

They probably found the lecture, which I gave at the U.S. Army War College the previous October, suspicious. But giving a course on virtuous leadership to senior American army officers hardly means I am a spy for the CIA.

☆

On October 19, 2012, I cross the threshold of FSB headquarters in the center of Moscow. The "organs" have scheduled a meeting for 10 a.m. I am prepared to tell them my life story. My future in Russia depends on the secret police—and the will of Almighty God, the Eternal Father.

I sense that my life is about to take a new turn. I feel this is not the end of my Russian way but merely the end of the beginning. I feel I am entering into one of the most rewarding periods of my life—even if, objectively, all is fraught with uncertainty. But that is a story for another time. For now, enough is enough.

# CONCLUSION

Havard is my family name. The French "Havard" is a corruption of the historic English name "Howard." Howard, according to family tradition, was an English knight who settled in France in the early 12th century.

Havard was the maiden name of my great-grandmother. It came to her male descendants accidentally after her death, as part of a scheme to aid my grandfather's flight from the USSR. His real name was Dianin—as is mine. The name invokes Diana, the goddess of the hunt and of the moon, according to Roman mythology.

But I very much love the name of my mother—Gedevanishvili—because it invokes the name of our ancestor Gedeon, whom I mentioned in the first page of this book: The Roman soldier of Georgian Jewish ethnicity who cast lots for the cloak of Christ at Golgotha. Gedeon is sinful humanity ransomed by the blood that it spills.

☆

Michael is my Christian name. It is the name I went by at school.

Alexandre is my middle name. It is the name I have gone by since my college days.

Alex is the name that was given to me in Finland because it is easier to decline than Alexandre (Finnish has 16 declinations).

Sasha is the diminutive of Alexandre. In Russia, I am called either Alex or Sasha.

At home, I have always been called "Tato."

Tato is my real name: It is the name God uses when He calls me. It is my essence.

1   Nikolai Berdyaev was a Russian religious and political philosopher.

2   Nikolai Berdyaev, *Dream and Reality: An Essay in Autobiography*.

3   The Gedevanishvili family descends directly from Gedeon. There are a number of Georgian historical sources that deal with the Crucifixion (it must be remembered that Georgia is the world's oldest Christian nation after Armenia). Those sources diverge on several points, but they all have this in common: Two brothers, Jews from Mtskheta, were present at the Crucifixion where they obtained the cloak of Christ and brought it back to the ancient Georgian capital.

4   The Russian name for a man's outer garment once commonly worn by men in the Caucasus, regardless of ethnicity. It was also adopted by the Kuban Cossacks.

5   Vladimir is 175 km (109 miles) NE of Moscow.

6   An *izba* is a traditional Russian country dwelling.

7   Alexander Borodin, "Letter of A. Borodin to A. Dianin and M. Goldstein," 17.09.1877, in *Letters of A. Borodin*.

8   Ibid, "Letter of A. Borodin to A. Dianin," 13.08.1877.

9   He will be secretly ordained a bishop in 1935 at the Roman Catholic Church of Saint Louis in Moscow and then become Apostolic Administrator for Leningrad and northern Russia. The Soviet authorities find out and expel him from the USSR three months later.

10   Anton Chekhov, "The Student," in *Selected Stories of Anton Chekhov*.

11   Peter Y. Chaadaev, *Philosophical Letters & Apology of a Madman*.

12   Peter Y. Chaadaev, "Letter to I. P. Turgenev," in *Polnoe sobranie sochineny* (complete works).

13   Vladimir Soloviev, *Three Powers*.

14   Nikolai Berdyaev, *The Russian Idea*.

15   Chaadaev, *Philosophical Letters & Apology of a Madman*.

16   Rene Laurentin and Ljudevit Rupcic, *Is the Virgin Mary Appearing at Medjugorje*.

17   *Savate,* as it is called in French, or *la boxe française,* is a traditional form of martial art combining elements of conventional boxing with graceful kicking techniques.

18   A book merchant who occupies a stall along the Seine River near Notre Dame Cathedral in Paris.

[19] Richard Wurmbrand died in 2001 in California.

[20] Richard Wurmbrand, *Tortured for Christ*.

[21] Olivier went on to have a very successful career in the hotel industry.

[22] World War I was raging at the time.

[23] These first two parts of the Fatima message—the vision of hell and revelations about Russia—were made public in 1942.

[24] This third part of the Fatima message—the vision of the martyred Church—was revealed in 2000 by Pope John Paul II.

[25] Fr. Antonio Maria Martins, SJ, *Memoirs and Letters of Sr. Lucia*.

[26] Josemaria Escriva, *The Way*.

[27] Grigoriy (Sergo) Ordzhonikidze (1886-1937). Georgian Communist, member of the Politburo, one of Joseph Stalin's main henchmen.

[28] Josemaria Escriva, *Way of the Cross*.

[29] Chaadaev, *Philosophical Letters & Apology of a Madman*.

[30] John Paul II, *Crossing the Threshold of Hope*.

[31] Vladimir Soloviev (Solovyov) (1853 –1900) was a Russian philosopher, theologian, poet, pamphleteer and literary critic, who played a significant role in the development of Russian philosophy and poetry at the end of the 19th century and in the spiritual renaissance of the early 20th century.

[32] Vladimir Soloviev, *The Heart of Reality: Essays on Beauty, Love and Ethics*.

[33] John Paul II, Speech on July 30, 2000.

[34] Fydor Dostoevsky, *A Writer's Diary*.

[35] During the siege of Paris by Attila the Hun in 451 A.D., St. Geneviève encouraged Parisians to resist the invasion with these famous words: "Let the men flee if they wish, if they are not capable of fighting. We women will pray to God so much that He will hear our supplications." In fact, Attila spared Paris.

[36] 36. Nikolai A. Berdyaev, *The Destiny of Russia (Sud'ba Rossii): Book I* (not translated into English).

[37] The Lycée militaire de Saint-Cyr is the most prestigious of the six *lycées* of the French Ministry of Defence.

[38] Finlandia Hall, Helsinki, June 5, 1989. Meeting with members of the Paasikivi Association.

[39] Aleksandr Solzhenitsyn, the Russian writer and author of *The Gulag Archipelago,* was arrested and expelled from the Soviet Union in February 1974. He took up residence in Cavendish, Vermont, where he remained until returning to Russia in the summer of 1995 after the fall of communism, the lifting of the charge of treason against him and the removal of all obstacles to the publication of his books in Russia.

[40] Jérôme Lejeune, "Child, Family, State: Scientific Progress and Human Rights," address at conference in Helsinki, April 1990.

[41] Russian for grandmother. It can be used when addressing any elderly woman not known by the speaker, but not in a situation requiring formality. When used in situations such as the one described above, the word does not imply a blood relationship and is considered affectionate.

[42] Alexandr Havard, *Virtuous Leadership: An Agenda for Personal Excellence.*

[43] In mid-December, daylight in Helsinki lasts a mere five hours.

[44] Escriva, *The Way.*

[45] Bishop Don Alvaro del Portillo was beatified on September 27, 2014 by Pope Francis.

[46] Nikolai Rerikh (or Roerich) (1874-1947) was a Russian painter, philosopher and archeologist of the emigration. He moved to India in 1923 and founded the Agni Yoga Society, which promoted theosophist ideas and would strongly influence the later New Age movement in Russia.

[47] Soviet People's Commissar for Social Welfare (1917–1918).

[48] Soviet People's Commissar of Enlightenment, responsible for culture and education (1917-1929).

[49] A hybrid Russian word meaning self-publishing. Samizdat publications circulated underground in the late Soviet period completely bypassing state censorship. Samizdat was an important vehicle for the dissemination of dissent, including works by and about Aleksandr Solzhenitsyn and Andrei Sakharov.

[50] Alik Zorin, "Artistic Creation in Light of the Teaching of Josemaria Escriva," presented in Rome on August 1, 2002 at The Greatness of Ordinary Life International Congress on the Occasion of the Centenary of the Birth of Saint Josemaria Escriva.

[51] Josemaria Escriva, *Furrow.*

[52] N. Anossova, *Adieu Russie.*

*ACKNOWLEDGMENTS*

I should like to thank Anthony T. Salvia,
for his generous contribution to every aspect of
*My Russian Way*, and Patrick J. McCloskey, for the
faith he showed in this book from the beginning.

To them, my endless gratitude.

**ALEXANDRE HAVARD** is the author of the Virtuous Leadership system and the founder of the Virtuous Leadership Institute (www.hvli.org). He was born in Paris and graduated from L'Université Paris Descartes, one of France's leading law schools. As a barrister, he has practiced law in several European countries. Havard now lives and works in Moscow where he teaches virtuous leadership to business executives and university students. He has presented to the senior management of the Russian Railways and the senior officers of the U.S. Army and U.S. Naval War Colleges. His books, *Virtuous Leadership* (Scepter Publishers, Inc., 2007) and *Created for Greatness: The Power of Magnanimity* (Scepter Publishers, Inc., 2011), have been translated into 15 languages.